Praise for *Brand Seduction*

"Daryl Weber's *Brand Seduction* is jam-packed with fascinating research and actionable insights. Weber shares the science of decision-making simply and clearly, which makes his book perfect for marketing practitioners, academics, and consumers alike. If you're fascinated by what makes consumers tick, this book's for you."
—Adam Alter, associate professor of Marketing at NYU Stern School of Business, New York Times best-selling author of *Drunk Tank Pink*

"The word 'brand' in marketing has become like the blank tile in Scrabble: people use it to mean anything they like. In this excellent book, Daryl does invaluable service in rooting the concept of a brand in proper scientific foundations."
—Rory Sutherland, vice chairman, Ogilvy & Mather UK

"Clever, creative, and jam packed with useful insights, *Brand Seduction* shows how our brain secretly shapes our choices in ways we may never have realized. A great tool for any marketing toolkit."
—Jonah Berger, Wharton professor and best-selling author of *Contagious and Invisible Influence*

"Brands exist in our brains. Daryl Weber delves into the non-conscious side of branding and provides a wealth of practical advice for brand-building at any scale."
—Roger Dooley, author of *Brainfluence*

BRAND

Seduction

HOW NEUROSCIENCE CAN HELP MARKETERS BUILD MEMORABLE BRANDS

———

DARYL WEBER

This edition first published in 2016 by Career Press, an imprint of
Red Wheel/Weiser, LLC
With offices at:
65 Parker Street, Suite 7
Newburyport, MA 01950
www.redwheelweiser.com
www.careerpress.com

ISBN: 978-1-63265-013-9
Library of Congress Cataloging-in-Publication Data
Names: Weber, Daryl, author.
Title: Brand seduction : how neuroscience can help marketers build
memorable brands / Daryl Weber.
Description: Wayne, NJ : Career Press, 2016. | Includes bibliographical
   references and index.
Identifiers: LCCN 2016001923 (print) | LCCN 2016011569 (ebook) |
ISBN 9781632650139 (paperback) | ISBN 9781632659859 (ebook)
Subjects: LCSH: Marketing. | Branding (Marketing)--Psychological
aspects. | BISAC: BUSINESS & ECONOMICS / Marketing / General. |
BUSINESS & ECONOMICS / Advertising & Promotion.
Classification: LCC HF5415 .W3573 2016 (print) | LCC HF5415
(ebook) | DDC
   658.8/27019--dc23
LC record available at http://lccn.loc.gov/2016001923

Cover design by Faceout Studio
Cover photograph © PLAINVIEW/istock
Interior by PerfecType, Nashville, TN

Printed in the United States of America
IBI
10 9 8 7 6 5 4 3 2 1

CONTENTS

PREFACE

For too many marketers, "science" is a four letter word. It squashes creativity, they say. Or that it's something for the market researchers to worry about. Worse, they claim it forces rules onto something that cannot be codified. Brand building is an art, they say, and science is its nemesis.

Because of this, a vast chasm exists between the science of how brands work and the marketers that could benefit from it. Most marketers I know would rather follow their gut and rely upon the small sample size of their past work experience.

This book is my attempt to dig deeper into the nature of brands, how they live in our minds, and to reveal how creative marketers can use this understanding to grow their brands.

Through the past decade I've worked at a global advertising agency, a boutique brand strategy and innovation consultancy, and in-house at one of the strongest brands in the world. I've been surrounded by experts in marketing and branding, but amazingly, *everyone seems to have a different idea of what a brand is and how to build one.*

At the same time, researchers have made great strides in our understanding of brands, brains, and the intersection of the two. There is still a long way to go, but we've learned a lot about decision-making, the role of the unconscious and emotions, how the brain perceives the outside world, how memory works, and much more that can be applied to understanding brands and consumer behavior.

I want to make this clear upfront: a lot of what I will describe may be hard to accept. We tend to resist ideas that contradict our common sense and everyday experiences. But I will show you how our common sense can sometimes be very wrong, and how our everyday experiences can mislead us. From there, we will see that much of how we assume consumers interact with brands is deeply flawed.

I urge you to be open minded. Based on the latest science, I will suggest new ways of thinking about some basic facets of our human experience: how we perceive the world, how our memories and emotions work, how we decide, and even question our notion of free will.

But wait, I thought this was a marketing book? It is, and I will use our understanding of the brain to build a new way of thinking about brands—what I'm calling the "Brand Fantasy." As you will see, the Brand Fantasy is the unconscious web of associations that together form a mental representation of a brand. This Fantasy is messy, irrational, abstract, and exists mostly below conscious awareness. It is what consumers are *really* buying when they choose a product.

This is where the science meets art. By diving into the unconscious feel of your brand, you can let go of strict, conscious guardrails and are free to explore the deep, hidden—and perhaps most powerful—aspects that may be lying dormant. Much like an artist, your job as a marketer becomes to share those latent feelings with the world. Rather than being a test at the end of the process, or a formulaic approach that must be strictly followed, I believe this kind of thinking can actually inspire greater creativity.

This book is organized into three sections. In Part I, we'll dive deep into the science with an eye-opening and fascinating look into how certain aspects of the brain work, with a focus on the unconscious. In Part II, we will use this understanding to build the idea of Brand Fantasies: what they are, how they exist in the mind, and how we can cultivate and mold them. In Part III, we will apply these ideas to brand building, advertising, market research, and product innovation.

By the end of this book, you'll know the brain for what it truly is: largely unconscious, quite lazy, driven by emotions, highly irrational, and more. You'll then see how we can build brands that fit with how the brain actually operates, rather than how we'd like it to.

Although there is still a long way to go in both brain and brand science, I do hope we can begin to close the gap between neuroscience and creative marketers. I hope you'll see how uncovering the unconscious side of brands can allow marketers to intimately know their brands on new levels and liberate and inspire them to explore the more abstract side of their brands.

As a companion to this book, you can refer to *www.daryl-weber.com* for links to further reading, videos, as well as tools and resources to help uncover, articulate, and build your own Brand Fantasies.

I hope you enjoy it.

INTRODUCTION:
THE MENTAL UNDERWORLD
OF BRANDS

"You can slam it down on the table. That's the best way I can describe it."

After struggling to find the words, that's how a 26-year-old guy in Los Angeles finally described what makes his preferred brand of vodka, Ketel One, different. He even mimicked the motion of plopping down the imaginary bottle in front of him, banging his fist onto the Formica table.

And he wasn't the only one. During the course of a series of focus groups across U.S. markets, many young men settled on the same descriptive motion: Ketel One was the brand that you could slam onto a table.

What did this mean? For one thing, it was another reminder of how people struggle to describe differences between brands and their relationships with them. In this case, the conversation attempted to dissect the difference between two leading premium vodkas: Grey Goose and Ketel One.

At first, these vodka drinkers insisted the two brands were the same in every way. They were both top-shelf, high-end brands. They were meant for the same kind of people—those who care about which vodka they choose and have a little more money to spend on the "better stuff." And of course, they defaulted to the one word most people use to describe any alcohol they like; they were both "smooth."

As the moderator, it was my job to pick apart these two brands and to figure out what was driving the recent growth behind Ketel One. The problem was, however, that even these guys that loyally purchased Ketel One had no idea why they did so.

I acknowledged I was splitting a hair and begged them to help me split that hair. Still, they had little rational or conscious explanation for what pulled them toward Ketel One and away from Grey Goose. They would say things like, "It's just the one I like," or "It's the one I've always picked." The brands were "pretty much the same."

So we pushed it further. We went beyond the rational discussion and verbal conversation to the messier world of emotions. We used projective techniques to tap into the *unconscious* associations with the two brands. We had these guys make up stories about the brands, create visual collages, and do association exercises. We got away from the conscious world of words and rational justifications, and began exploring the deeper elements of their relationships with each brand.

Suddenly, stark differences began to surface. For Ketel One, a bold, masculine theme emerged. They told stories of the brand at poker nights. They showed images of boxers with bulging muscles. They placed it alongside uber-masculine symbols like scotch, cigars, and steak houses. They showed weathered, bearded mountain men. This is not what you'd normally think of for the sleek, ultra-premium vodka category, and nothing like what they had just been describing.

Grey Goose, for these Ketel One drinkers, was delicate. It was fancy, a bit pretentious, and slightly snobby. It wasn't quite feminine, but definitely more gender-neutral compared to the masculinity they saw in Ketel One.

In other words, Grey Goose needs to be gingerly placed on the table, whereas Ketel One could be slammed.

We also spoke with loyal Grey Goose drinkers who saw things very differently. They saw Grey Goose as the best of the best. It was for those with class, style, and taste. It was perfect and anything else was a step down. For them, Ketel One was the less sophisticated option that lacked the beautifully sleek, polished style they connected with in Grey Goose.

So what's going on here? Functionally and rationally, both brands occupy the same space in both sets of drinkers' minds. They are both high-end, smooth, premium vodkas. But deep down, the two brands have very different essences. They convey different associations, different emotional connections, different moods, personalities, and aspirations.

They seem the same, but they *feel* very different.

And that *feeling* toward each brand was clearly what split the group and what drove some to be loyal to one over the other. To some, Grey Goose had the sleek style and sophistication they identify with. To others, Ketel One embodied more of what they aspire to—bold masculinity.

Now, I realize very few men will freely say this. They may be reluctant to admit it, or they may not even be aware of it. But for most men, alcohol choices, especially in the context of a bar scene and dating/pickup culture, are often judged on whether they are manly or not (how many times have you heard someone's fruity, colorful drink choice be described as "girly"?). So without much of a leap, you can see these guys wanted a drink that displayed some masculinity, probably to themselves as much as to others. And when not drinking an obviously masculine choice like a brown liquor, Ketel One gave them at least a touch of that feeling.

The Brand Fantasy

This unconscious feeling toward a brand is what I call the "Brand Fantasy." It's a messy network of associations that get woven together to form an unconscious representation of the brand. It's a primordial soup made up of fleeting images, abstract thoughts, and nuanced emotions that, for the most part, live below our conscious awareness.

The Brand Fantasy underpins the "gut feeling" you have toward something. It can be positive, in that it draws you toward something, neutral, or negative, in that it pushes you away. As we will see, this hidden combination of associations can powerfully influence our decision-making and behavior, all while unbeknownst to us.

I call it a "Fantasy" because, ideally, a brand should represent something that people aspire toward. It could be a feeling they want to have, something they want to be associated with and connected to, or provide a taste of the life they'd like to live. To use a made-up marketing word, it is "aspirational," meaning people aspire to it. I also like the word "fantasy" because it feels ethereal and dreamlike, which fits with the emotional and unconscious nature of these brand associations.

For the case of Ketel One drinkers, the Ketel One Brand Fantasy contains a mix of bold masculinity, combined with classic authenticity, and a vague sense of foreignness, of being from somewhere else. It feels rugged and robust, classic and with heritage, true to itself and confident, while still having a premium style. To these loyal Ketel One drinkers, this is the Brand's Fantasy. Most didn't consciously think about it this way, but it was there below the surface, slyly asserting its influence.

So where did this collection of perceptions come from? For Ketel One, the answer became clear: it formed almost entirely from the bottle itself. The brand had a long-running ad campaign that depicted short letters written in the gothic font of the brand (they all started with "Dear Ketel One Drinker . . ."), but almost none of the respondents we had spoken to had ever seen it (or couldn't recall seeing it). By far, most of their brand associations came from the packaging, combined with its premium pricing and the settings in which they experienced the brand.

The Ketel One drinkers described the bottle's thick glass, bold edges, and masculine shoulders. It felt sturdy and robust. The graphics and font made it feel old and gave it a history. Unlike many other premium vodka brands at the time, it wasn't trying to be sleek, cold, and minimalist. It boldly went in a new direction. That made the brand feel confident; it stayed true to itself and didn't try to be something it wasn't.

But this was all a very "zoomed out" view of the bottle. Amazingly, despite being regular drinkers of the brand, very few knew how to correctly spell it, often misspelling it as "Kettle One." They also had never read the label which clearly described the year it was founded (1691) and the country of origin (Holland, but most guessed Russia, Poland, or

Though the liquid inside is nearly identical, the look of these two bottles make the brands feel very different.

Germany). The truth is that they didn't care. It was enough to create the Fantasy to know that it was old and from somewhere else, and they could ascertain both of those things from a fleeting glance at the bottle from across a crowded bar. The same was true for Grey Goose—the intricate painting on the bottle, the elegant cursive font, the gently sloped curves of the bottle, and artfully frosted glass all made it feel too delicate and pretentious to some, whereas the same elements were interpreted as stylish and premium to others.

Brand Fantasy vs. Brand "Positioning"

We've now hit on my definition of a brand. Put simply, a brand is a collection of associations that exist in the minds of consumers. Many of these associations can be conscious, like the product or service itself, its function, the design, the advertisements, and so on. But that is just the tip of the proverbial iceberg. Many of the powerful feelings and emotional undertones that we automatically and unconsciously connect with a brand exists below our awareness. It's this rich constellation of mental associations—both unconscious and conscious—that I am calling the Brand Fantasy.

If you're reading this book, you are probably familiar with the now ubiquitous marketing term "positioning." Coined by Al Ries and Jack Trout, the word first appeared in the 1970s in a series of articles in the magazine *Advertising Age* and later in their now classic book, *Positioning*.[1] The main idea is that every brand can only own one simple idea in consumers' minds. One brand, one idea.

The way they describe it is that this one idea is usually the physical product description the brand can own. For example, Philadelphia is cream cheese, Dial is soap, and Kleenex is tissues. Those brands should not try to expand outside of those categories as consumers already have strict mental walls set up for what each of those brands can do. If you saw Kleenex making paper towels, for example, what would you think? Probably that they'd be weak, flimsy, tissue-like paper towels. Or take the Clorox Company that makes their famous bleach, but also manufactures Hidden Valley Ranch salad dressing. Who wants to think that Clorox makes Ranch dressing? Those two things definitely do not mix.

As a brand consultant for well over a decade, I have seen countless tools from major marketers intended to capture a brand's positioning on paper. These can take many forms such as a one-sentence positioning statement, a brand house, a brand architecture, a brand onion (think layers), a brand wheel, a brand pyramid, and more. All of these can be effective at summarizing a brand and giving everyone who touches the brand a clear set of guidelines to follow.

But all of these positioning tools have one major drawback: they do not reflect the reality of how consumers experience brands. They focus on the conscious side of brands, while almost entirely ignoring the powerful unconscious side. This is a big mistake.

It is certainly important to know who your target audience is, the insight you want to tap into, and what the functional and emotional benefits are, but isn't it also important to viscerally experience and *feel* the brand the way your consumers do?

The Brand Fantasy is my attempt to start thinking of brands closer to how they actually exist in people's minds. This rich, 3D expression filled with emotions and loose associations is much messier than the simple positioning documents we're used to, but it's closer to what actually pushes consumers toward a purchasing decision.

We want brands to be simple. Marketers are people too, and people like simple things. So we reduce the brand down to its essential components or even a "one word equity." But the mind is complex. Our conscious mind wants to have things simple, but the unconscious mind has many layers and it's in these layers that our motivating gut feelings form and bubble up.

*M*ost marketers focus on the conscious side of brands, at the expense of the unconscious side. Even when they talk about reaching consumers "emotionally," they are still focusing on conscious elements. The Brand Fantasy explores the powerful, but usually hidden, unconscious side of brands.

In a way, I'd argue that the Brand Fantasy can actually be simpler than often wordy and complex positioning statements. The Fantasy creates one coherent whole that weaves together many pieces of a brand in a way that can be easily felt at a visceral level.

In psychology, the term *gestalt* refers to how the brain prefers to seek out the whole of something, rather than the individual parts. The brain wants to quickly categorize something and figure out its function, so it will auto-fill in what it needs to create a complete picture that it can make sense of. In much the same way, the Fantasy represents the whole of the brand—it's the complete picture—beyond just the conscious pieces that fit nicely on a page.

The value of a Fantasy

The power of these underlying connections we have to brands becomes obvious when we look at private label brands vs. their branded counterparts. In pharmaceuticals, though private label brands (store brands) have a large and often growing share of the market, it's amazing that the much more expensive branded products still sell as well as they do. In CVS, you can buy 300 tablets of Advil for $20.99, or $0.70 per tablet. The CVS-branded ibuprofen—which contains the *exact* same medicine at the same dosage, and is held to the same safety and effectiveness standards by the FDA—costs only $0.24 per tablet. When you put the Advil name on the bottle, the same product becomes three times more expensive.

This kind of brand power goes beyond the rational. Our unconscious mind tells us we know and trust the Advil brand. We feel positively toward it, so we use that as a shortcut to our decision. The CVS bottle has virtually no brand—no set of emotions or feelings attached to it. There's no Fantasy. Though we can consciously override our emotional pull toward the branded product and choose the cheaper option, many of us just feel a little better about the Advil, so that's what ends up in our basket.

We will get deeper into the science of emotions and decision-making in the following chapters, but for now, we can see that these gut feelings have a huge impact on quick decisions at the shelf in the supermarket, at the drugstore, or even online. Our feelings serve as shortcuts; we don't want to think about the choice too much.

Taking a cue from the fashion world

Fashion and luxury brands build compelling Brand Fantasies better than any other industry. They've built entire empires off of rich brand associations and emotions, often with a complete lack of reference to materials, physical attributes, or any kind of rational message. These categories often get thought of as not being "strategic" in the typical sense of having a clear brand message, role of the product, or point of view, but maybe they know something we don't.

Fashion brands know the power of tapping latent emotional desires and often have a clearer sense of the fantasy they want to convey and own. They are quite happy to show their product in alternate realities that hint at a fantasy world we'd want to be a part of. They know the mood, the feeling, the dream world that they want to connect with and that becomes their marketing strategy. They know this is how consumers choose which brand in these categories to associate themselves with, so the Fantasy becomes their focus.

Think of a fashion brand. Can you imagine what the dream world of J. Crew looks like? How about Brooks Brothers, Polo, or Abercrombie? Why does the turquoise box from Tiffany's hold such power over so many women? Each one of these has a clear, distinct, and rich brand culture connected to it.

They've created their own brand worlds. For each you could imagine a planet; you could see the people in them, what they look like, what their jobs are, what cars they drive, and more. They've only hinted at this world through their products, ads, catalogs, stores, celebrity endorsements, and so on, but it's there, subconsciously associated to their brands. They've built the worlds; now it's up to us to choose if we want to join it.

Burberry has built a strong brand with prestige, cachet, and style. Of course, it produces high quality products that are on trend, but does it have a message, a unique selling proposition, or a functional positioning in the market? It has none of these, and it doesn't matter. It has a boldly consistent brand look and feel that creates a relevant and aspirational fantasy, and that is more powerful than any rational attribute.

The strongest brands are built on the strongest Fantasies

The strongest brands in the world today use this philosophy, whether they realize it or not.

Think of Coca-Cola, who have owned the top spot on the branding agency Interbrand's list of most valuable brands for the past 13 years (until it was bumped by Apple in 2013). According to Coca-Cola's advertising, the brand stands for happiness. When you open a bottle, you "open happiness," as the recent tagline says.

But that doesn't begin to tell the whole story of the brand. For sure, happiness is a key component of its brand and is a great emotion for a brand to connect with and own, but what about all the other associations that make Coca-Cola the globally loved icon it has been for decades? The brand also has strong ties to nostalgia—memories of growing up with it and drinking it with family. It's all-American, a taste of America for other countries, and a classic that harkens back to the good ol' days for those in the U.S. It's optimistic and uplifting. It's a simple pleasure, in good times and bad. It's for everyone, rich or poor. It's a rock of our culture—enduring and steadfast no matter what goes on around it.

All of these ideas combine to create its Brand Fantasy, and all of them contribute to Coca-Cola's unprecedented brand strength and longevity. Just think, how does that deep, rich, and emotional fantasy compare to a fantasy for Pepsi? It doesn't.

Take Nike, another iconic brand that manages to consistently maintain its cool through the years. With a smart and creative mix of cutting-edge product design and innovation, PR and publicity with top athletes, celebrity endorsements, and envelope-pushing advertising, Nike's image stays a step ahead. Its Brand Fantasy feels forward thinking, motivating (with its famous tagline, "Just Do It"), and athletic—but for everyone, whether you are an athlete or not.

Although Nike still dominates, the athletic apparel company Under Armour has made significant inroads into the market with a strong and differentiating Fantasy of its own. Born out of American football, Under Armour owns a tougher, edgier, more hardcore place in the market. It can make almost anyone feel on some level like the toughest NFL linebacker, even if for only a moment. This is a clear and tight Brand Fantasy that makes it stand apart.

Smaller brands can build strong Brand Fantasies as well. Think of how the brand Method upended the household cleaning products category with an entirely new look and feel. This disruptive new Fantasy changed the rules for what mattered in the category from cleaning efficacy alone to design and a modern, eco-conscious aesthetic.

Or take Lululemon, the super-premium line of yoga apparel that shot to the top of the category in a few short years. The brand captured the essence of yoga, which is about pampering and loving yourself, feeling free, relaxed, and Zen-like.

No discussion of brands would be complete without a look at Apple, the reigning king of brands. As we all have probably seen, the Apple brand breeds loyalty so strong that it borders on the fanatic. Apple "fan boys" will debate rumors of new product launches for months or even years in advance, will wait in line for hours, will buy almost anything from the company, and will pay nearly any price for it. And they will do all this while barely pausing to give the competition a second look (unless of course to disparage them).

I will take a fresh look at Apple through the lens of a Brand Fantasy. The company's products scream innovation, delivered with elegance, simplicity, and modern design. Apple sparks its users' creativity, and lets them feel in with the cool crowd. Despite being hugely popular, and now actually overtaking the grand daddy Microsoft in many areas, they still maintain a sense of counterculture and a rebellious, groundbreaking attitude.

Samsung can shout all it wants to about the better features on its mobile phones. But if it's not an iPhone, many people will not even listen. Look at the Brand Fantasy behind Apple. How would you describe Samsung in comparison? Maybe that it's Korean, and has high quality products. But it pretty much ends there.

As Kevin Roberts, the CEO of global advertising network Saatchi & Saatchi wrote in his book *Lovemarks*, brands this strong create "loyalty beyond reason."[2] People remain loyal to brands like this even when it's not rational, even in the face of competing information. They love it and don't need to waste time or energy listening to anything else.

Yes, we're talking about the sizzle, not the steak

In many ways, the Fantasy is an illusion. It's not real. It's a dream world that brands create. It exists in our unconscious and in our feelings. But that is powerful. In many ways, these fantasies add real value to the products and to our lives. A fake Rolex will give most of us less pleasure than wearing the real thing. Take the Nike swoosh off a sneaker and it loses some of its magic.

You can actually enjoy a purchase more and get more value from it if it has emotional value to you. In this way, brands can add real value, beyond their physical product attributes. (For an entertaining look at how brands add value by changing our perceptions, check out Rory Sutherland's TED Talk entitled "Life Lessons from an Ad Man.")

In later chapters we will discuss "top down processing," where the higher order processing of the brain can actually influence how we perceive the world. The classic example of this in marketing is the Pepsi Challenge. When participants tasted Pepsi and Coke blindly, Pepsi was preferred. But when respondents could see the brand, Coke was preferred. In this case, the Coca-Cola brand was powerful enough to make the product actually taste better. And when talking about taste, perception is the only reality.

> *The* unconscious elements that together form a Brand Fantasy aren't just fluff; they add real value and can greatly enhance the experience for consumers.

Think of it as similar to your relationships with people. You can't rationally woo someone into loving you. You can't argue it, or use well-reasoned, logical points. You just have to feel it. Imagine trying to write a "positioning statement" or "brand architecture" for someone you love. You could probably think of some descriptors and key traits of their personality, but would that ever do it justice? Could that ever capture all the nuanced feelings and associations you have with the person? Could it even be put into words?

When we put brands into those few words, we try to do exactly that. We reduce a rich and abstract set of feelings into a few lines that make us happy that we "understand" the brand. But they usually leave out many of the most important and motivating elements.

Now, the marketing veterans among you might be thinking, "Sure, we all know now that tapping into emotions is critical for brands to compete today." But that's not what I'm saying. The Brand's Fantasy is much more than, say, the emotional benefit we ascribe to it (like happiness for Coca-Cola or freedom for Harley Davidson). As we will see in the next few chapters, I believe we are actually thinking about emotions in the wrong way. It's not about standing for or owning an emotion, or even making your ads more emotional. It's about creating a *gut feeling* toward the product that makes your brand the preferred option.

So it's not about directly communicating an emotion to your consumers. Instead, you are trying to build the right associations with your brand that together build the right feeling toward the brand.

You also might be thinking, is this just the brand's equity, personality, tonality, or maybe its "archetype"? The answer is yes; but it is all these things and more, all wrapped together. The personality of a brand is usually relegated to a side note, or left for the agency creatives to figure out. I'm arguing here that these types of traits, along with the many other unconscious associations of a brand, are in fact *central and critical* to how consumers feel toward your brand. I want to move them from the periphery of branding to part of the core of what a brand is and how we build one.

Hopefully, this Introduction gave you a sense for the idea of the Brand Fantasy and the critical role of unconscious brand associations. The next section will dive into some of the surprising and strange ways our brains work, and how the Brand Fantasy gets formed and lives in our minds.

PART I

The Brain-Brand Connection

Introduction to Part I:
The Brain-Brand Connection

Does anyone think ads work on them? Most consumers—and especially marketers—feel they're immune to the siren calls of marketing. We wouldn't be so foolish as to see or hear something from a brand and then blindly follow along. We're thinking, rational creatures after all, capable of making our own choices. Or so we think. The mind is a tricky thing. We may be very aware of our own state of being—what we see, hear, think, and feel—but what we can't see, or know directly, is how our brain is working. We can't see behind the scenes. We have conscious access to just the tip of the iceberg of information—what's most necessary to know in the moment—but there is so much more going on. As marketers, it behooves us to take a peek behind the curtain, to see what makes us who we are, and makes us do what we do. To do that, we must understand the brain. There is a tendency in our culture to draw a sharp divide between the physical and the mental, between the flesh of the body, the "brain," and the intangible, thinking "mind." Without getting too philosophical or religious, for the purposes of this book we'll think of the brain and mind as inextricably linked, and really as one and the same thing. In Part I, the goal will be to introduce some of the basic processes for how the brain works so we can build on that understanding in the following sections. Obviously, neuroscience and its related fields are immensely complex. We will barely scratch the surface in these few pages, but I will try to stick to the most pertinent, fascinating, and thought-provoking facts to help us build the story for how brands live in our brains. Here's a quick tour for what we'll go through in Part I:

Chapter 1 will start by getting you acquainted with the three-pound lump in your head. We'll look at how consciousness evolved to help keep us alive (not to navigate the modern world). We'll then explore how we perceive the world around us—how we effortlessly create a beautiful and coherent mental image of the world, and how this is often not the reality we think it is.

Then we'll look at the role of attention in Chapter 2 and how it relates to brands. Attention is coveted currency among advertisers, but we'll see how our assumptions about it are often wrong.

In Chapter 3, we'll look at the different types of memory—particularly the unconscious ones—and how we experience memory can be very different from reality.

We will then dive into the true meaning of emotions in Chapter 4, how they are often misunderstood—especially among marketers—and how they influence our decision-making.

Lastly, Chapter 5 will go deeper into how we humans make decisions, how much of what influences our decisions is outside of our awareness, and how irrational we really are.

To me, there is nothing more fascinating than the strange and amazing ways in which the brain works, and I hope you will gain an appreciation for this as well. If you'd like to go deeper, there are other books that go much further into the science of the brain in relation to brands and marketing, and you can find my recommendations for those at *www.daryl-weber.com*.

CHAPTER 1

Beauty is in the Brain of the Beholder

How Brands Enter the Mind

*Our perception of the world is a
fantasy that coincides with reality.*
—Chris Frith

Oh, the brain, one of the greatest frontiers in science today. Although we have come a long way in understanding many of its basic processes and functions, there is still so much we don't know. Some philosophers believe we can't use our brains to ever fully understand the brain (how can the brain ever really know itself?), but I believe in the coming decades we'll continue to chip away at this vastly complex and awe-inspiring organ, and that our understanding of it will begin to influence many aspects of life, from education, to economics, to law, and yes, marketing.

This chapter will serve as a brief introduction to the amazing wonder inside our heads. For the science-phobes among you, I hope you find it fascinating and somewhat illuminating. And don't worry, there won't be a test.

Let's peek under the microscope

Try this: make fists with both of your hands and put them together in front of you (you may have to put this book down, but that's okay, I'll wait). That double fist is roughly the size of your brain. There it is. That's it. It even has two hemispheres like your brain.

Within that small space exists everything about your very being. It's who you are, how you sense the world, how you move, how you breathe, and how you feel. Everything you've ever learned and everything you've ever experienced, and so much more, are all in that little three-pound lump that's about the same size as an average cauliflower.

Inside that lump we have a mix of brain cells, mainly neurons and their supporting structures called glial cells. Though glial cells greatly outnumber neurons, the real action happens in the neurons, so let's get to know them.

A single neuron looks a bit like a tiny tree—it has a long trunk and many branches that extend out. Now, we have a lot of neurons in our brains; the latest estimates say about 86–100 billion of them. For context, that's close to half of the stars in our Milky Way galaxy. But amazingly, that's only the start of it.

Neurons connect to their neighboring neurons at intersections called synapses. And it's in these connection points where the numbers get really, really big.

Every one of those 100 billion neurons can have thousands of synapses with other neurons. If we assume each neuron has 1000 synapses (a conservative estimate, given that many have 10,000 connections or more), we can see that 86 billion multiplied by 1000 is going to have a lot of zeros. It would be a 10 with 14 zeros after it, in fact. Many estimates put the number of synaptic connections in the average human brain in the hundreds of trillions, and up to one thousand trillion unique, individual connection points. One. Thousand. Trillion.

It's hard for us to fathom numbers so big. That's why news reporters will often use metaphors like football fields for distances, or the amount of times something can wrap around the earth. So let's try one here. If we use our Milky Way galaxy again, which astronomers estimate to have around 400 billion stars, we see that the cerebral cortex alone (just the outermost layer of the brain) has more synaptic connections than the number of stars in 1,500 Milky Way galaxies. In fact, just one cubic centimeter of brain has more connections than stars in our galaxy, and the total length of the neuronal "wires" in the brain has been estimated to be in the millions of miles.

Some estimates say the amount of synaptic connections translates to anywhere from 1–100 terabytes of computer data. For comparison, the entire content of the Library of Congress has about 10 terabytes of data.

Okay, Okay, you get it. The connections and information processing in the brain is insanely vast.

I'm emphasizing the incredible epicness here for a reason: it's in this vast array of connections that the magic of the brain happens. We don't know for sure, but a leading theory is that our experience of consciousness arises out of this massive connectivity between neurons. These single cells, by turning each other on and off in enormous networks, seem to be the basis for learning, memory, and conscious thought—much like how a computer turns strings of 1s and 0s into complex software programs. Amazing, right?

Dr. Sebastian Seung, a brilliant professor of computational neuroscience at MIT, has coined the term "connectome" to refer to how this array of neural networks makes us who we are. In his words, "I am my connectome." This means that all of your memories and everything that makes you, you, is embedded as information within your connectome. He believes that our genome may determine physical attributes, like eye color, and even aspects of our personality, but that the biological basis for our identity lies in our connectome.

There are now groups of researchers working on actually mapping this connectome, much like how the human genome has now been mapped. This is an extraordinarily immense undertaking; remember, thousands of trillions of connections have to be mapped, neuron by neuron, and synapse by synapse. But if and when they succeed, it could show us the inner workings of our personality, memory, intelligence, and mental disorders. It even hints at a science

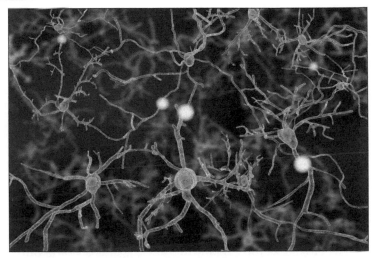

Neurons can have tens of thousands of connections to other neurons, creating a vast "connectome" that may hold the biological basis for our sense of self and identity.

fiction future where we can "upload" our consciousness to computers.

It's also important to note that the connectome is not a static, fixed thing. It is living, breathing, and dynamic. Your experiences change your connectome. As we grow and learn, it changes with us. Even just thinking changes it. This is indeed what learning is—the strengthening and rewiring of neuronal connections.

The classic phrase from Psych 101 classes is that neurons that "fire together, wire together." Meaning, the more we repeat a particular action or thought, the stronger those neural connections are, and the easier the action becomes. This seems to be the biological basis for learning and memory. It's why practicing something makes you better and why you get rusty when you stop. In a way, it's like working a muscle.

Your brain was built for survival, not for Walmart

What are brains for? Why do we have them at all?

You might think they're for thinking, reasoning, and feeling. We use them for that now, and those abilities seemed to have evolved to help our ancestors survive in their hostile world (coordinating hunts, social skills, learning what's dangerous, planning ahead, and so on). But it seems brains evolved in the animal kingdom for one purpose: movement.

Only animals that move have brains. Take the humble (and unfortunately named) sea squirt, an aquatic animal that starts life as a swimming tadpole-like creature. But once it finds a suitable place to attach itself, it stays there for life and actually then digests its own brain and spinal cord, as they're no longer needed.

Our brains exist for one purpose: to move us. We're now using this ancient machinery for entirely different purposes than what evolution intended.

As neuroscientist Daniel Wolpert says, "To understand movement is to understand the whole brain."[1] He believes all of the functions of the brain—memory, cognition, sensory processing—are there for the specific reason of *taking action*. All the amazing things we can now do with our brains originally evolved to help us do something in the real world.

This means you can't think of the brain as a solitary unit, separate from the body. The brain is intimately connected to the body in everything it does. We work as one complete system.

It also means that most things we do in today's world—reading, driving, doing math, and shopping for brands and products—are all ways we have repurposed our ancestral neural machinery to do something it was not originally intended to do.

For example, we humans are notoriously bad at statistics. We don't have good judgment or feel for things that deal with large numbers. So we tend to fear flying and not driving, when statistically driving is much more dangerous. Or we fall victim to the "gambler's fallacy" at casinos when we think surely the next hand will be a good one because our previous five hands were so bad (of course, your current hand doesn't know or care about your last hand). It's also why we like to make pretty charts rather than look at spreadsheets of numbers. The same numbers from a spreadsheet suddenly make more sense to us when put into a chart, as that fits with how our brains have evolved.

We're all barely conscious

Looking at it from this evolutionary perspective helps us see why the brain works the way it does. And it shows that our experience of consciousness—seeing, feeling, moving our way through the world—is really only a tiny fraction of what our brains do.

Think about it; at any given moment, your brain is doing countless actions to keep you alive. Right now, it's keeping you breathing, balanced and upright, your heart pumping, monitoring the world around you, building and repairing tissue, fighting off diseases, and on and on. My brain doesn't trust me to keep track of all that, and who can blame it? I wouldn't trust myself either.

Evolution programmed our bodies to run on autopilot for everything that it possibly can. A pregnant woman even creates an entire new human being without any blueprints or directions. Her body does it on its own.

We assume we're in conscious control of our actions, but this is the misleading story our brains tell us. In reality, we're driven by unconscious, irrational drivers far more than we realize.

So, in a way, we're mostly unconscious creatures. We move through the world with a sense of complete control over who we are and what we do, but how much of that is an illusion created by the brain? We assume our conscious experience in our daily lives tells us the whole story, but it's not even close. It actually tells us a *misleading* story.

As you will see throughout Part I, much of our conscious experience of reality is flawed—it's an illusion our mind creates to keep us functioning. We may think we have a clear sense of how our perceptions, attention, memory, emotions, and decisions work and behave the way they do, but in reality, we don't.

As you can see, this two-fist sized, three-pound lump in your head is pretty complex, and we've barely scratched the surface. Somehow, in ways we are just beginning to understand, our experience of consciousness arises out of this complexity. All of our feelings, thoughts, beliefs, and everything else we experience is somehow tied to the processes of those neurons, working together in neural networks that together form the different structures of the brain. It's a wonderful and amazing system, and for the most part it works incredibly well.

In the next few chapters, we will dive into different aspects of the mysterious and surprising ways in which the brain works. These will give you a better understanding for how brands enter the mind, are stored in our memory, and ultimately influence our decisions and behaviors.

How the brain takes in the world

Put down this book for a second, and take a moment to look around you. Actually, don't just look, really take in the entire scene. What do you hear, smell, and feel? (I hope you're not reading this in a bathroom.)

In that quick second, and really, before you even did it, your mind created a complete mental picture of the world around you. Even if you're not paying attention to it, your brain knows where you are, it's monitoring the sounds around you for any potential dangers, and you can see, with great detail and clarity, everything in your vicinity. You do it without thinking or exerting any effort at all. It just happens.

But how does it happen? How does scattered light bouncing all over get from objects in the world to a clear image in your mind? How do undulating sound waves in the air become the sounds of music, of approaching footsteps, or even the words of language?

These are no easy feats. And yet we do them every second of every day, without even trying. In general, we take our senses for granted, unless something goes wrong.

In the rest of this chapter we'll explore how our brains make sense of, and navigate through, the world around us. We will look at how human perception doesn't work the way it seems to, how much of what we experience is really a mental illusion, and how our beliefs and expectations shape what we perceive.

As marketers, we craft communications intended to reach consumers, touch them emotionally, and ultimately influence their purchasing behavior. But before any of that can happen, it must first find a path into the mind. Let's explore that path.

We see with our brains, not with our eyes

We see with our eyes, right? It would certainly seem that way. After all, that's where the light enters, and when I put on glasses my vision improves.

Although the eye is an amazing piece of evolutionary engineering, it is only the beginning. We see in what appears to be great precision and clarity, with rich detail and color. But this is not even close to what your eye "sees."

The raw image from light hitting the retina on the back of your eye is, to put it nicely, a total mess. The image appears upside down, backward, blurry, two dimensional, and even includes a pretty large blind spot smack in the middle of it (reminds me of some nights in college). But unless we've had way too much to drink, that's not at all what we see when we look out into the world.

So it's up to the brain to make up the difference. It takes this incomplete and shoddy image, and turns it into the beautiful world we see. *It fills in the gaps.* Your eyes take this raw visual mess hitting your retina and converts it into neuronal (electrical) signals that can be sent to your brain. There, things can come into focus.

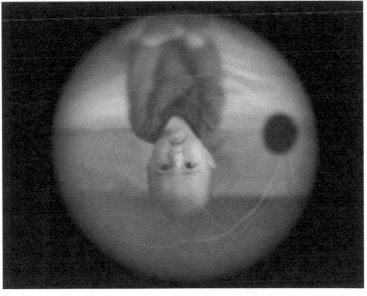

The raw image that hits your retina is nothing like what we actually "see."

A German doctor and physicist named Hermann von Helmholtz first made the realization that the eye's image quality was so poor, it seemed to make vision impossible. To make up for this low quality image, he theorized that our brain must be making a set of assumptions—what he called "unconscious inferences"—that are basically educated guesses on what is out in the world based on our prior experience. For example, if a ball appears to be getting smaller and smaller, the brain will assume that it is moving further away, not getting smaller, as that is more likely to be true in the world.

Scientists call this idea "top-down processing." It means that our perceptions come more *down* from the brain than they come *up* from the eyes (or any sensory organ). Our brain uses these inferences and systems of understanding the world to fill in the incomplete information we get from our senses. These systems are called *schemas* and we begin creating them as infants. They typically come in very handy, as we don't want to see the world totally fresh every time we look out, but should use our prior knowledge about how the world works to *interpret* what we see, not just see it.

So really, our brain is doing the seeing and most of what we think we are seeing in the world is actually an interpretation—or really an illusion—created by our brains.

Take the clichéd philosophy question, "If a tree falls in the forest, and no one is around to hear it, does it make a sound?" If we look at it from this neuroscience point of view, the answer becomes clear: no. The tree may push out waves of air as it falls, but it takes a brain to turn those airwaves into the sound of a tree falling. Without a brain, they are just lost, wandering waves of air, not a sound. Sorry tree.

The same is true for our perception of color. We hold a deep belief that things in the world are a color. It is in their very nature to be that color. Bananas are yellow. Leaves are green. But what if colors are creations of the mind and don't exist out in the world? In fact, leaves absorb every color *except* green. They reflect that one wavelength of light and our brains interpret that to be green.

And just because we see something a certain way, that doesn't mean that accurately reflects what it is. Humans can only see across a narrow band of light, what we call the visible spectrum. Bees, for example, can see infrared light, so many flowers that look one way to us, often look very different to bees. Who's to say whose interpretation is correct?

Your brain does all this instantaneously. It takes that messy image on the retina and makes it make sense. It fills in the large blind spot near the center of your visual field (caused by the optic nerve in each eye), fills in color in your peripheral vision (you actually have no real color perception in your peripheral vision!), adjusts for the movements of the eye itself, recognizes objects and gives them meaning, scans for faces, and much more. Oh, and it makes the whole thing three dimensional. That's pretty amazing, right?

These inferences the brain makes are right most of the time; if they didn't work well, they wouldn't have helped us survive and evolve. But the mind can easily be tricked, and it's in these tricks that we see the assumptions the mind is making.

For example, when you move your eyes to look from one place to another (called saccades), you don't see the world move (even though the image has just swooshed across your retina). You don't even see any blurring. Your brain accounts for the fact that you moved your eye and automatically subtracts the movement. But if you gently touch your eyeball on the lid and give it a nudge with your finger, the world does seem to move. Your brain doesn't account for this, as this is not a normal occurrence.

Or take the experiment done by psychologist George Stratton, who wore special glasses that inverted the image on his retina so that it was actually right side up. Not surprisingly, at first his brain flipped this image again so that he saw everything upside down, but after only a few days his brain had flipped the image back so that he was now seeing normal again—but through upside down glasses. And of course, when he took the glasses off, everything was again upside down until his brain flipped it back.

This is how optical illusions work. They play our brain's assumptions against us, to trick the mind. Amazingly, illusions work even when we know for sure that what we are seeing isn't right. Our conscious mind cannot override

You may have seen the heated online controversy in 2015 surrounding a photo of a blue and black (or is it white and gold?) dress. The image of that dress was right on a perceptual boundary where, depending on your brain's personal schema, you'd see it as white and gold or as blue and black. Your brain's assumptions make you see it one way and you can't change it.

the power of these unconscious inferences, even when we know it's wrong and want to change it.

Or teh fcat taht you can esialy raed tihs stenence eevn wehn teh wdros are jmulbed.

The brain looks for patterns and recognizes words by the expectations set. It sees the context, the meaning, the first and last letters, and then just fills in the rest of the word.

This isn't just true for vision; we can even create and observe audio illusions. Take this example from how we process spoken language: when we hear a sentence spoken aloud, our brain automatically parses the stream of sound into discrete words, even though those spaces do not actually exist.

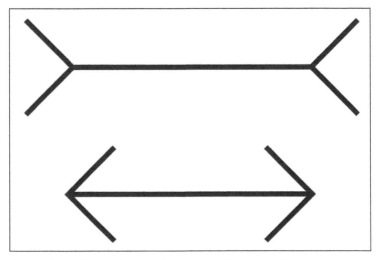

Even though you know these two lines are the same length, it's very difficult to override your unconscious inferences.

This mental illusion is so compelling that people often find it hard to believe. But it's true. If you could see the sound wave of a spoken sentence, there would not be any blank spaces between the words, like the spaces between the words you see on this page. Itwouldlookmorelikethis—a single continuous sound stream with no real breaks.

But our conscious experience (when it's a language we know) is that we hear each word distinctly and separate on its own. If you listen to a foreign language that you have no familiarity with, you can see the effect; you will have no idea where one word ends and the next begins. When you know the language, your mind puts the spaces in, without any conscious effort.

So really, when we perceive something, we don't see, hear, or feel how it exists exactly, perfectly in the world. In a way, perception can be thought of more as *construction*— a back and forth dance between what our external inputs are telling us and what our brain's expectations want us to experience.

We see what we expect to see and taste what we expect to taste

What goes into making a great tasting wine?

You might think the quality of the grapes, the terroir, the skills of the winemaker, and so on. These all play an important role, but as we'll see, taste is about much more than what's inside the bottle.

What about the marketing of the product? Can a more elegant bottle label influence the taste? How about a more well-known brand name? Or what about the price?

Could these elements actually change how we perceive the physical taste of the wine? As we have seen, if our brains are doing the tasting, and constructing the experience of the taste based on prior experiences, expectations, and context (your mood, the people around you), then it wouldn't be too much of a stretch to think that these elements could play a role.

That's exactly what a number of studies on wine tasting have sought to understand. Take the 2008 study at the California Institute of Technology run by Hilke Plassman. Plassman wanted to see if marketing activities can affect our experience of wine, both from a subjective self-reported perspective, and even from a physical, neuronal perspective in the brain.[2]

Do you have a favorite brand of vodka, or a favorite type of wine? Do you think you would know it by taste alone? Well, let's find out. Have a friend pour your preferred brand and a similar competitor so that you don't know which is which. Then, without looking, see if you can taste the difference, and pick out your favorite. For most people in most categories with similar products, this proves much harder than they would first expect. Without the information from the brand to help set our expectations, our taste and smell receptors can only go so far.

Wine-loving participants in the study were given five wines to taste, and were told they were taking part in a study to understand taste perception for different flavors (not really true, but don't be mad, researchers lie to participants all the time). Participants tasted the wines while inside an fMRI machine so that their brains could be scanned in real time. Not the most relaxing wine drinking environment, but it did the job.

They were also shown the prices of the wine, ranging from seemingly cheap $10 glasses to expensive $90 glasses. They also gave the participants the same wine twice, but once it was shown to be $10, and the other time $90.

At first, they found what you might expect. Most participants were not able to tell that they had the same wine twice and self-reported that the more expensive wines tasted better, even when it was the same wine from the very same bottle.

But self-reports can be influenced by many factors; perhaps the participants wanted to sound cultured and thought the more expensive wine *should* taste better, so they reported it that way. So let's look at what was happening inside their brains while they sipped.

If we look at the primary taste areas of the brain, we don't see any difference between the alleged $10 bottle and the $90 bottle. Both reacted the same way, which makes sense as physically it is the same wine.

But when we look at the medial orbitofrontal cortex— an area of the brain strongly associated with experiences of pleasure—we see stark differences. For the $10 bottle, there was very little brain activation in this area. But when the same bottle appeared to be worth $90, this area of the brain became very active, showing that the participants were drawing *real* pleasure from the experience that they did not have from the $10 bottle.

So the physical taste parts of the brain saw the wine as the same, but the pleasure parts of the brain—because of the expectations set by the price—had a very different experience. The price tag of the wine did indeed have real physiological influence over how the wine tasted.

They expected the wine to taste better, so it actually did.

You might be thinking, sure, but these were amateurs. Wouldn't professional wine tasters be able to tell the difference? In fact, many studies have shown the same effect with world renowned wine experts as well.[3] Even these highly trained pros were not immune to the effect of their own expectations.

> *W*hat we perceive is not a direct reflection of reality. The brain interprets incoming signals based on expectations and makes its best guess at reality.

Many studies show similar findings related to price, as well as other aspects of our expectations influencing our perceptions of reality. Studies have shown that your ability to pronounce a winery's name (referred to in psychology as "fluency") influences taste perception, whereas *harder* to pronounce names seem to taste better, but in more utilitarian products, easier to pronounce names look to be higher quality.[4]

One study played French or German music in a wine store, causing people to buy more French wine if French music was playing, or German wine if that country's music was playing, despite being unaware of the music playing or its influence on them.[5]

Or take this study done by Dan Ariely, professor of behavioral economics at Duke University and author of the best-selling book *Predictably Irrational*. He gave people at a bar the choice between a regular beer or one that had vinegar added to it. As you might expect, most people said they hated the vinegar beer and chose the regular one. When he didn't tell them that one had vinegar in it, however, and just asked which of these do you prefer, most chose the beer with the added vinegar. Apparently, vinegar actually makes beer taste better, but not if you know it.

In Ariely's words, "Our pre-conceptions of reality actually affect how we interpret reality."[6]

This is where things get interesting to us as marketers. If, in many ways, it's our brains that do the seeing, hearing, and tasting, and does so by using pre-existing patterns and inferences, where do these inferences come from? How do they affect perception of brands, and how are those perceptions encoded in memory, and involved with actions and behaviors?

To answer these questions, let's look at how what we perceive gets encoded in the brain.

We don't just see something, we see what it means

Say you're walking down a supermarket aisle and pick up a can of Campbell's soup that you haven't seen before. You hold it in your hand and look at the label.

First, as we've seen, the soup hits your retina as an upside down, blurry image with a blind spot in it (not what the designers intended). There, transducers (the rods and cones) in your eye convert the visual stimuli into electrical signals that head straight to the brain.

First stop, the thalamus. The thalamus sits deep within the middle of the brain. It acts as a kind of switchboard for incoming sensory signals. Every sensory system (except the olfactory system, for smells) goes through the thalamus and then gets sent off to its specific processing area of the brain.

But incoming signals are also sent to a small almond-shaped structure on either side of the brain called the *amygdala*. The amygdala combines sensory inputs and "tags" this input with an emotional coloring. It gives a meaning to the input and tells us if we should be scared of it or look for more of it. This emotional coloring gives us that "gut feeling" of whether something is good or bad.

The amygdala is also where memory and emotion combine. It works closely with its neighbor, the hippocampus, which helps encode the details and facts of an event into long-term memory. Together, these code the experience or behavior as pleasing or traumatic and either can create an emotional memory that lasts a lifetime.

So we don't just perceive the physical attributes of whatever we're looking at, we see what it *means* to us. We instantly categorize it (a chair, a person, a tree) and know if it represents a threat or positive reward with an emotional coloring (is that a branch or a snake on the ground?). This process is called "conceptualization." It means we know what the thing we are looking at is and what, if anything, we should do about it.

Scientists also refer to the principle of "gestalt" to explain this idea. It means that when the brain perceives something it makes it into a whole, rather than the sum of its parts. We don't see wheels, tires, windows, and metal. We see a car. We don't see legs, fur, adorable eyes, and floppy ears. We see a puppy. The gestalt is the whole, which exists as a different thing in the mind to its parts.

Let's apply this to our can of Campbell's soup. In an instant, the image is processed by the thalamus, through the amygdala and hippocampus, and many other parts of the brain. Through this process, the physical incoming stimuli of the image are combined with our past experience of the Campbell's brand. We immediately know what it is and how we feel toward it. Maybe we have warm, fuzzy memories of our mom making chicken soup when we were sick. Maybe we've had a gooey grilled cheese with tomato soup on a rainy day. We then might notice the name of this new flavor, the look of the design, the price, and even the feel of the can.

All of these elements combine to influence how we see this new can of soup. It gives us a gut feeling on whether or not we want to drop it into our cart or not. We probably won't think about it for too long, or with much effort, but will "go with our gut" if we feel like we want it or not. In Procter & Gamble language, this is the "moment of truth" where the consumer makes the buying decision. It's the moment when all of the marketing efforts culminate into a make-or-break decision.

This is the power of the Brand Fantasy—it creates and guides the consumer's gut feeling toward the brand. It can get the can in the shopping cart or get it put back on the shelf.

———

I hope this chapter shed some light onto how our minds take in and process the world around us. Clearly, our expectations, beliefs, and prior experiences exert great influence on and shape how we perceive new information. We don't just see the world as it is, but how we believe and expect it to be. And we don't see individual objects on their own, but we see their meaning, the feelings connected to them, and other related concepts.

For marketers, this has important implications for how we reach consumers through packaging, design, user experience, and communications. We need to ensure that we're building and creating the right associations and connections with our brands in consumers' minds with every touch point.

Takeaways

- The brain evolved to help us survive the hostile life of hunter-gatherers, not to navigate modern life. We are using our ancient machinery for new purposes.
- One leading theory states that our conscious experience arises out of our "connectome"—the vast array of neuronal connections in the brain.

- The brain is closely intertwined with the body, we cannot separate them, as neither works without the other.
- We aren't aware of the vast majority of our brain's activities, and much of what we do experience is actually more of an illusion than reality.
- We see with our brains, not with our eyes. Due to "top down processing," our brains fill in the gaps in our perceptions based on assumptions and expectations.
- We don't perceive things exactly how they are in reality. Much of what we perceive is an illusion created by the brain's assumptions. Most of the time these are right, but we can sometimes be tricked, and we can't help it, even when we know.
- Everything we perceive gets encoded with meaning and emotion, automatically. We don't just see something; we see what it is, what it means to us, and how we feel about it.
- When we see a brand, our brain uses its past experience to build assumptions and expectations to interpret what it's seeing, which influences how we feel toward the brand.

CHAPTER 2

Do I Have Your Attention?

Why it May Not Matter As Much As You Think

Have you ever been in a loud, noisy place when suddenly you hear your name from across the room?

You turn and look, even though you weren't paying attention to the conversation over there, and couldn't hear anything else they were saying. Somehow, your name pops out over the din and you hear it over everything else.

Sound familiar? This is the famous "cocktail party effect," and it demonstrates a key principle on how your brain pays attention to the world.

Most of the time, you're focusing on one thing—the task at hand. It could be the person across from you, the TV, reading this book, or work you're doing. Though you may get distracted every so often, in general, our energy and attention center on one thing at a time. Psychologists call this your "spotlight of attention." You shine your cognitive spotlight on one thing, and everything else sits in the dark.

This makes intuitive sense and fits with how we think of our attention working—one thing at a time. As anyone who has tried to "multi-task" knows, you can't really do two things that require your attention at once; you have to switch back and forth between them.

But how, then, do you hear your name from across a noisy room if it sits hidden outside of your spotlight? As it turns out, your brain constantly monitors and scans way more than you are aware of. Evolutionarily, this makes sense as you would need to quickly become aware of and react to any approaching threat. But your brain only gives "you" access to the bit of information most relevant at the time. Otherwise, you'd be bombarded with tons of stimuli and unable to focus on any one thing.

This again shows how there is so much happening in our subconscious that we are unaware of. It's kept hidden to allow us to move through the world with ease and not be bothered by every little thing the brain must do at all times.

So although you think you are listening to just the person in front of you at the party and blocking out all the noise around you, your brain is listening to that noise, and in a way to every conversation, for anything that might be relevant to you. Then when it hears your name, it instantly brings it to your attention into the "spotlight" of consciousness.

Attention, then, is more complex than it might first appear. It's not simply that we pay attention to one thing and only that gets into our mind. As we will see in this chapter, attention works at different levels and in different ways, and each of these have an effect on how we perceive, encode, and react to marketing communications and brands.

The power of low-involvement processing

For most marketers, attention is king. We think attention is the currency of the consumer and we're in a battle to compete for our share of it.

We talk about "breaking through the clutter," or needing to reach "distracted consumers," and the issues of "multi-screen viewing." We assume we need to break our audience out of what they are doing and get them to pay attention to our message. This holds true for any medium or type of communication: digital, social, TV, print, out-of-home, radio, and so on.

After all, if they don't pay attention to our message, how can we ever hope to reach them, affect their opinions, and ultimately their purchasing behavior?

Well, there may be another way.

We assume consumers need to pay attention to our messages because that's how we learn most things in life. When you go to school, you concentrate on something, try to remember it, take notes, study and review it later, all with the hopes of keeping the new ideas in memory at least long enough to pass the test.

In cases like this, you are highly motivated to learn and retain the information, and devote energy to focusing on it and storing it. This is called *high-involvement processing*.

But that's not how most brand learning takes place. Unless you work in marketing, most people don't feel that learning about brands is that important, so they don't put much effort into it. They tend to assume most products are about the same, or they pretty much know what is being advertised, or that they're being "sold to," so they don't pay much attention to it.

Brands also tend to reach us while we are in relaxed states, like casually watching TV, scrolling through Facebook, listening to the radio, or flipping pages of a magazine. We're not paying close attention because we're just trying to be entertained, relax, and generally "shut down" from all the concentrating we do in the rest of our lives.

This type of shallow attention is called *low-involvement processing*, and it's critical to how much of our learning about brands happens.

Dr. Robert Heath, a former advertising executive and current professor and researcher at the University of Bath in the UK, leads the charge on the importance of low-involvement processing and its role in brand learning. Through his two excellent books, *The Hidden Power of Advertising* (2001) and *Seducing the Subconscious: The Psychology of Emotional Influence in Advertising* (2012), and in his published research papers, he details how low-involvement processing is key to understanding how consumers build their unconscious feelings toward brands.[1]

I want to make one thing clear upfront: getting focused, concentrated attention from consumers still does work, and is still desirable. If you can get consumers to stop what they are doing and really pay attention to your messages—and engage in what psychologists call "active learning"—then you have the best chance at changing their perceptions and winning them over.

However, the reality is this rarely happens. Though marketers constantly try, consumers still process the vast majority of advertising with little interest or engagement.

The Super Bowl is a notable exception. Here, many of us watch specifically for the ads and pay a lot of attention to them, but that is a once-a-year occurrence. We may also occasionally "opt-in" or choose to see advertising messages, especially online. But most of the time, let's be honest, they're just ads and we tune most of it out.

When consumers only give you partial attention with shallow processing, they're not processing much of the rational, conscious messages we try to get across. Instead, they get the overall tone and feel of a brand, and that is what gets stored into memory.

*T*hough marketers put most of their effort into crafting conscious messages, the reality is, most advertising only gets partial attention via shallow processing. That means the conscious message rarely gets encoded, but the general gist and tone of the ad remains in memory.

Have you ever had the experience of driving a familiar route, only to realize when you arrive at the destination that you don't remember much or any of the drive? Maybe you were on the phone (hands-free of course), listening to music, or just lost in your own thoughts. Somehow you managed to drive safely, but didn't seem to process it much or encode it into memory.

That is shallow processing in action. Your brain was able to watch the road, change lanes, make turns, all while most of your conscious attention was somewhere else. Of course, if something happens—say someone cuts you off—your attention would be immediately brought back to driving so you could react.

We generally move through the world in a state of shallow processing. We don't actively try to learn or remember everything we do or encounter; there would just be way too much to process and remember. Our brain likes to keep our conscious mind free and clear of all of this so we can focus on what's important in the moment.

We now know that when you're doing nearly anything, your brain is constantly processing everything around you, even if you're not aware of it. You don't know your brain is doing it because this kind of processing is fully automatic and unconscious (just like the cocktail party effect). It happens in the background.

But here's the kicker. Our brains don't just monitor our surroundings when we're not paying attention, but they actually *learn* from them as well. Psychologists call this *implicit learning*, and it's happening all the time. You are actually learning without being aware of it. (Take that, school teachers who thought I wasn't paying attention!)

Fergus Craik and Robert Lockhart are two cognitive psychologists who first studied and developed the idea of different levels of processing attention. Although at first they assumed that shallow processing would lead to very little recall and rapid forgetting, later studies from them and others have shown that learning created via shallow processing created *implicit memories*—memories that you didn't even know you had—and that these memories could actually last for months.[2]

Cognitive psychologists now widely accept the idea of low-involvement processing and the implicit learning that goes along with it. In particular, these traits are widely understood to be how shallow processing and implicit learning work:

It seems most of our brand associations are built through low-involvement processing. Though marketers don't give it much thought, we're encountering brands all the time and every interaction is automatically processed in a very durable and long-lasting way.

- It's fast, automatic, and happening all the time.
- It requires zero attention and doesn't take away from other tasks.
- You're not aware of them, and they're not even available to consciousness if you try.
- It's unavoidable; you can't help but have them enter your subconscious.

Other researchers have shown that "automatic processes suffer no capacity limitations . . . and are very hard to modify once they have been learned."[3] That's right, not only do they slip in easily, all the time, and undetected, but it seems we can store an endless amount of implicit associations, and they last for very long and are hard to change.

Again, it makes evolutionary sense that our minds would work this way. As we navigate the world, we should be learning from our experiences and actions, but this learning shouldn't take away from what we need to be concentrating on.

Brands are constantly sneaking into our minds

Like we did in the last chapter, take a moment to look around you again, but this time check for how many branded products you see.

I'm writing on a MacBook Air, have a Motorola cell phone next to me, am wearing a North Face jacket, and drinking a smartwater. And that's just on or right near me. If I look further, at other people, or take a short walk, I'll see many more brands.

We encounter brands all the time. We often think modern consumers are bombarded with advertising, but really we see brands in many forms and in many places, not just in ads or on shelves. And as we've seen with implicit learning, each of these encounters with a brand—*regardless of how incidental or minor they may seem*—sneakily burrows its way into your brain, whether you realize it or not.

So as we go about our daily lives, paying our conscious attention to many different things, all of these tiny brand exposures subtly sneak into our subconscious, collecting and amassing themselves into a set of associations, perceptions, and beliefs connected to the brand.

Every single time you encounter a brand, a little association gets added to the pile. It can be where you saw it, who it was with, or what you were doing. These experiences all subtly and quietly influence our subconscious feeling toward that brand and, most of the time, we have no idea it is happening.

These associations gained from implicit learning can be very durable, long-lasting memories. It's why well-established brands have such a hard time changing their perceptions— these feelings and associations run deep, and don't want to be changed.

$\mathcal{T}$ry this the next time you're watching TV with at least one other person. Wait for an ad to come on, and try to slyly notice how much attention they pay to the commercial. Then, once it ends (assuming they stayed in the room, and they're not on a device or fast forwarding it!), ask them about the ad. What happened? What brand was the ad for? See how much of the ad, even if they were staring right at it, consciously got in and was remembered.

Often, people struggle to remember what an ad was for, even seconds after they saw it. They were just tuned out. But, as we've seen, that doesn't mean the ad didn't subtly influence their perceptions and feelings toward the brand on a deeper, subconscious level.

Let's look at an example: Jack Daniel's whiskey. For most people, this brand conjures up rugged, tough, masculine imagery. It's a badass, rock n' roll brand with some real edge to it. It's fiercely independent and authentic. Today, these associations seem almost inherent in the product itself—Jack Daniel's just *is* badass. But where did this rich set of perceptions and associations—this Brand Fantasy—come from?

Do you remember seeing ads for it? Most people I've asked can't specifically recall any particular ad, campaign, or even a tagline for Jack Daniel's, even though the brand has been advertising for decades. In other words, they don't have any explicit recall of it, and probably didn't engage in any active learning if they did see the ads. Clearly, the Jack Daniel's brand presence goes far beyond advertising.

As a teenager, I had a poster of Guns N' Roses hanging on the wall in my room where the band members were all skeletons (that's normal, right?). And there was the lead guitar player, Slash, wearing his trademark top hat, smoking a cigarette, and holding in his hand, what else, a bottle of Jack.

You've probably seen the bottle at rock concerts, with Frank Sinatra and the rest of the Rat Pack, in music videos, with biker gangs, and on and on. You may have been in bars where groups of guys were taking shots of it. You've seen the bold bottle shape, the masculine name and black label design, the price, and so on.

As we can now see, your mind was shallow processing all of the information without your awareness, and encoding the information with a bit of relevant context. As we saw in the last chapter, your thalamus, amygdala, hippocampus, and other parts of your brain "tagged" and conceptualized each experience with meaning and an emotional coding so that you could learn from it.

So when you combine all of these little pieces, you're left with a pretty robust, complete, and strongly ingrained sense for what the Jack Daniel's brand is about. You didn't look for it. You didn't pay attention to it, or try to remember it. It just happened, without you realizing, as you go through life.

This is its Brand Fantasy, and it gets created without any mental effort. That is the power of low-involvement processing and implicit learning at work.

"Subliminal messaging"—fact or fiction?

It seems only appropriate that a book about the unconscious aspects of brands would touch on the controversial subject of subliminal advertising. So here we go.

You may have heard about the infamous study that spawned the idea of subliminal advertising in our cultural consciousness. It was a fake study in fact, done by a man named James Vicary in 1957. He claimed that by flashing the words "Eat Popcorn" and "Drink Coke" at super fast rates (too fast to be consciously perceived) during the screening of a movie, he was able to increase sales for both products.

The "study" turned out to be a hoax, but it sparked widespread discussion, worry, and occasional panic about the possibility of hidden messages slipping into our minds without our permission.

Today, any ethical marketer would fully reject the idea of trying to slip anything past a consumer without their knowledge, of course. There are government regulations in the U.S. that make subliminal messaging illegal, but I've never heard of an actual case of this happening, and don't think any legitimate business would engage in it.

But the case I am building in this book is all about how we unconsciously learn about brands, and how this can influence our eventual decision-making and purchasing behavior. So, in a way, everything we see from a brand works on both conscious and subconscious levels. There are the conscious messages we can see, talk about, and recall. Then there are all the other associations we build and connect with brands that we don't even realize we are making. Our implicit learning takes these pieces in, conceptualizes them with meaning, tags them with emotions, and adds them to the connections we have about a brand—all without our awareness.

So, in a way, all advertising can be considered subliminal. An ad may have a conscious, rational message, and it may even feel very emotional. But what can be even more powerful, and have a longer-lasting effect, are the unconscious associations it creates in us.

This is true for any kind of brand communication. Where you see a brand or product, the environment it's in, the color of the fonts or backgrounds, the people you see with it, and so on, all play a part in shaping our sense for that brand. Though the ad may be explicitly talking about a functional, rational, or even an emotional message, all of these other aspects of the brand seep into our subconscious and mold our feeling toward it.

These other aspects are called "meta-communication." The colors, fonts, music, and where it's seen, for instance, all influence our perception of the brand and the ad, usually without us paying any direct attention to them. Everything about an advertisement communicates, and every part adds to our associations (more on this in Chapter 10).

We may or may not give much conscious attention to "what" is being said, but "how" it is being communicated is seeping into our unconscious via implicit learning.

You might be thinking, "Sure, but there's no way these things influence *me*. I know why I buy the products I buy. Maybe all those 'People of Wal-Mart' get tricked, but I'm too smart for that."

Well, sorry Einstein, but it's true. As psychologists learn more and more about how our consciousness, emotions, and decision-making work, the more we realize we are less in control than we think we are. There are tons of studies in neuroscience and psychology that show how we humans fall prey to influences outside of our awareness.

Although the rational brain can override our feelings, we tend to go with our gut. And it's these unconscious associations that build that gut feeling and help steer us toward a decision.

Can you actually have too much attention?

You've probably had this happen: you see an ad on TV, laugh at it, and think it's great. You even mention it to your friends. But, what was that ad for?

It turns out this is pretty common. In a move of attentional jiu jitsu, the advertisers managed to get your attention, but redirected it to the wrong thing.

Psychologists call this *inattentional blindness*. It's when something is visible in plain sight, but you just don't see it because you're engaged in another task. Although your eyes are working fine, your brain just doesn't see it (this effect is also called perceptual blindness).

The classic study illustrating this effect was done by Daniel Simons and Christopher Chabris.[4] If you haven't seen it, I encourage you to look up the "Monkey Business Illusion" on YouTube and play along with the experiment in the video before reading on.

As this and many similar experiments show, something can capture your attention so strongly that it blinds you to other things going on, even when those other things are incredibly obvious, like a man in a gorilla suit waving his arms at you!

---

*M*agicians are masters of inattentional blindness. They manipulate your attention with the art of misdirection—they get you to focus on one thing, where you think the action is, so that they can do something else. They know how human attention works and use it to easily and consistently trick us. For more on this, check out master pickpocket Apollo Robbins explaining the idea of misdirection of attention (with live demonstrations!) in his amazing TED Talk.

In marketing, we often try so hard to get consumers to stop and look at our communications that we end up guiding their attention to the wrong thing and away from the brand and message. Some examples of this are when sexy, provocative images are shown, or something is particularly funny or outrageous. They might grab the viewer's attention, but at what cost?

The second potential problem with trying to gain direct attention is the idea of counter-argument. This idea was first presented by Sharon Shavitt and Timothy Brock, and has been expanded upon by Robert Heath.[5] It's the idea that the more consumers think about a claim or idea in an advertisement, the easier it is for them to argue against that claim.

In other words, when marketers do end up winning consumers' attention, it can cause the consumers to start picking holes in it. As anyone who has watched consumers in a focus group knows, give people enough time and they will find everything wrong with your ad, product, or idea.

However, this means the opposite is also true—that when we don't pay much attention, we're less likely to counter-argue and, therefore, more likely to accept the brand's claims. As we've seen, unless you work in advertising or marketing, you're probably not going to spend much effort or thought arguing against ads.

So, in a way, more relaxed, less focused attention can actually help let marketers' messages slip through into consumers' brains without much of a fight, whereas direct, focused attention can cause consumers to put up their defenses.

In this chapter, I hope I've given you new ways to think about attention, and a clearer understanding for how consumers learn about brands.

Although the ideas of implicit learning through shallow processing are well established and recognized in psychology, for marketers, they still prove hard to accept. As do many findings in psychology, it goes against our common sense and intuition. It seems natural that we would need to get conscious attention to get consumers to hear our message.

Though that can work, it is highly unlikely and happens only rarely. It seems a better strategy would be to understand how the vast majority of brand learning works, and create brand materials and communications that work with our low-involvement processing and implicit learning. This is what I hope the Brand Fantasy model can help with.

Remember that we can, and should, still play to the conscious mind, but we must also take into account all the processing that is going on below the surface, as these perceptions may be even stronger, more enduring, and more influential on decision-making.

Takeaways

- Most people (unless you work in marketing) tend to only pay partial, shallow attention to brands and their communications. This type of attention is called low-involvement processing.

- We are constantly scanning and learning from our environments through automatic shallow processing.
- Although we're not paying conscious attention to it, our brains are learning and making unconscious associations all the time through what is called implicit learning. This is how we create and develop most of our associations with brands.
- In a way, all advertising is subliminal, because all messaging will have both conscious and subconscious elements. Brand associations seep into our subconscious, mostly without us realizing it.
- It is possible to have too much attention to marketing materials, as they can cause inattentional blindness for the brand and message, or counter-arguments against your message.

CHAPTER 3

Remember That?

How Brands Live in
Our Memory

What did you eat for breakfast today?

That's pretty easy to remember, right? Even though you didn't actively try to process it at the time or make a "mental note" of it, it happened recently enough that we can go back in our mind and look at what went on this morning.

Generally, this is how we see memory working. It seems we have this amazing ability to step back in time and take a mental peek into our past. Our memory feels like a file cabinet; we go back to the right time, pick the right file, and recall what happened.

And memories are more than just a list of events. They're what make us, us. Our memories shape who we are, our identity, and how we see ourselves. In a way, we are our memories.

But as we've seen before, our conscious experience of something is usually not the whole story and often misleading.

Memory is no different. Memory works in mysterious ways, most of which are unavailable to conscious introspection. Although our memories may feel fundamental to who we are, in many ways they are more fiction than fact.

In this chapter we will get acquainted with the real ways memory works and see how it can subtly and slyly influence our beliefs and behaviors. We'll look at how different kinds of memories are created, how they can often be wrong, the power of implicit memory, as well as the concepts of associative networks and priming. We will then look at how this relates to our memories, feelings, and beliefs toward brands.

The stuff of memory

What is a memory? When you thought about what you ate for breakfast this morning, what actually happened in your brain?

Though we don't know for sure, scientists are beginning to better understand how the brain encodes and recalls memories. If you remember (get it?) from Chapter 1, whenever we learn something new, we're creating new neuronal connections and strengthening existing connections. As we said, neurons that "fire together, wire together," meaning when one fires, the other neuron becomes more likely to fire (the technical term for this is *long-term potentiation*). The two neurons' relationship grows stronger and they become more closely connected.

But to learn something in the real world, far more than just two neurons get involved. Neuroscientists now believe memories exist in large networks of interconnected neurons, distributed throughout the brain. So whenever we learn something new, vast networks of neurons are created, altered, or strengthened.

It's kind of like working a muscle. The more we use a muscle, the stronger it gets. Similarly, the more we rehearse, recall, or practice something, the stronger the connections in those neural networks get. The analogy goes even further: we now know that as certain parts of the brain get used more, they actually get physically larger. Just like a muscle, it grows as it gets stronger. This is because the neurons in that region of the brain are growing more connections with their neighbors, and that takes up more space.

One study looked at the brains of British taxicab drivers that were experts at navigating the notoriously circuitous and complex streets of London. They found that veteran drivers had significantly larger hippocampi than the average person (the hippocampus is a structure deep in the brain involved in spatial navigation, as well as consolidation of memories).

Another study showed that string instrument players, like violinists, have a larger part of their cortex devoted to the motor control of the fingers in their left hand than did control participants. They also saw that the amount of cortical real estate devoted to the left hand digits directly correlated to how many years they had been playing their instrument. The more they had played and practiced, the larger this motor control area grew.

So the brain physically changes and responds to our learning. Neuroscientists call this the brain's "plasticity"— its amazing ability to constantly adapt and reorganize itself based on our experiences, environment, behavior, and even what we think.

As we grow and change as people, our brains grow and change with us.

We don't rewind, we reconstruct

When we think about our past, it feels like we mentally fly back in time. It seems we hit rewind in our minds and relive the moment.

Although this may be our conscious experience of memory, the truth is very different.

A leading theory among cognitive psychologists is that whenever we recall a memory, we are actually *reconstructing* that memory, rather than finding and picking out a precise replica of what happened.

It seems a memory isn't stored as a single whole, but rather as disparate pieces, spread throughout the brain. When we recall the memory, our brain puts the pieces back together, and in the process it automatically fills in any missing holes and gaps. As we saw in Chapter 1, this is just like how our visual system automatically fills in the gaps from the rough and incomplete visual information presented to the eyes. Our brain takes the incomplete pieces and glues it back together in the way that makes the most sense. We don't notice it happening; we just get the final mental image that seems to be an accurate representation of what happened, just like we don't notice the imperfections and holes in our vision. Our brains hide it from us so that we have the best and most useful representation to work with.

So memories are stored as networks of connections, distributed throughout the brain. Psychologists call these memory networks *engrams*. When we want to recall the memory, we activate the network of connections and reconstruct the memory by pulling the disparate pieces together.

Giep Franzen and Margot Bouwman, authors of the book *The Mental World of Brands*, call the neuronal network of memories for brands the *brand engram*.[1] A brand engram is the vast web of interconnecting neurons that represent all of the thoughts and memories for the brand. This is a nice neural corollary for the idea of the Brand Fantasy.

This process of reconstruction of memories makes evolutionary sense. Our brains evolved to be able to predict the future based on past events, rather than to keep track of the past. Recalling the past in vivid detail would likely not help survival too much, but it would be highly useful to use the past to make predictions on what might come next.

Though this reconstruction process gives us the illusion of a complete and accurate memory, the truth is our memory deceives us more than we realize. As Elizabeth Loftus, a brilliant psychologist who studies false memory, says: "Memory works like a Wikipedia page: you can go in there and change it, and so can other people."

Many of her studies show how eyewitness testimony in courtroom trials can often be very wrong, despite the witness claiming to be "100% sure" of his or her account. One famous study showed how slight rewording of a question can cause drastic changes to a witness's account. They showed respondents a video tape of two cars crashing into each other and then asked them either: "How fast were the cars going when they *hit* each other?" or "How fast were the cars going when they *smashed* into each other?"[2]

In the first part of the experiment, respondents who were asked about the cars "smashing" into each other estimated the cars were going much faster than those who heard the word "hit." That's interesting, but somewhat expected, and could be explained by the question wording changing the respondents' responses, but not necessarily their memory of the event. That's where the second part of the experiment comes in.

They then waited a week, and asked the same respondents 10 more questions about the film of the cars crashing, without showing the film again. Mixed in with the questions was the one they were interested in: "Did you see any broken glass?" There was no broken glass in the film. But for nearly half of those that had the "smashed" question a week ago, they said they had seen glass. Almost no one in the "hit" or the control group said they saw glass. This shows that their memory for the event had been changed, simply by changing one word, in one question, asked one week ago.

This is just one example of how our memory is more fragile and more fictional than we like to believe. As many other studies show, our memories can often be altered or completely false memories can be added. Not only do we not know that it's happening, but we often "remember" new details in these events, and will feel totally confident that they're true. Sometimes, you can't even trust yourself.

It seems the way in which we recall a memory also plays a key role in how we remember it. The act of remembering can change the memory itself. It has even been shown that the more times you retrieve a memory, the more you alter it. Each time you retrieve a memory, you may slightly tweak or distort parts of it without realizing it. So some of your fondest memories that you often think of, could actually be some of the least true!

Clearly, our conscious memory is far more fallible than what our experience tells us. Memories are reconstructed each time we recall something and are influenced by many factors at the time of remembering. This certainly holds true for how we remember and think about brands—they can often be false or misleading, based on our preconceptions of

---

*P*reconceptions and beliefs influence memory. In a study by Elizabeth Loftus, executed through *Slate* magazine online, readers were asked if they remembered seeing events from the past decade. One picture showed President Obama shaking the hand of Iranian President Mahmoud Ahmadinejad. About 26 percent said they "remembered," and talked about how they felt even though it never happened. *Slate* Photoshopped the image. Politically conservative readers were more likely to "remember" the handshake than liberals. For liberals, the effect happened with an image of George W. Bush vacationing at his ranch during Hurricane Katrina, which never happened.

---

the brand, our current experience, the act of remembering, and more.

But that is for our conscious memory. Let's now peek below the conscious surface.

The hidden side of memory

When we think about memories, we typically think of consciously recalling events, people, facts, or where we put our keys. Generally, these types of memory are called "explicit memory," but there are many more layers to memory than just that.

Hiding beneath the surface of consciousness lies the world of *implicit memory*. We experience implicit memory every day when we do things we had to learn and work at in the past, but no longer have to think about, like how to drive a car or hold a pencil. Like they say with riding a bike, once you learn it you never forget. It just comes back to you. This shows how powerful and durable these implicit memories can be.

Implicit memory has been shown not just to be procedural, but conceptual as well—meaning we can learn new ideas in this way, not just actions and movements. As we saw in the previous chapter on attention, we can learn new concepts through implicit learning, which is a subconscious, inattentive form of learning. These concepts are then stored implicitly in implicit memory.

A few studies done by the great memory researcher Daniel Schacter and his colleagues looked at the interesting case of amnesic patients who had lost their explicit memory, but could still create new implicit memories. In these studies, amnesic patients were able to get better at completing certain tasks—they were learning and improving—despite having no explicit recall of ever having done the task before.[3]

Furthermore, it was clear that the patients had not just retained the stimuli, but the *meaning* of it as well, even though they couldn't consciously recall it. And these implicit memories were shown to last for a very long time.

These findings suggest that as we implicitly learn about things in the world, we are also storing their meaning in our minds without being consciously aware of them. This shows that brands—and the meaning we assign to them—don't just sneak into the mind, but also stay there for a very long time, all without us realizing it.

———————

*T*hink about a favorite brand of yours. Now, try to break down at least some of the associations you have with that brand. Close your eyes, and really think about the personality and feeling of the brand. What do you associate with it? This can be anything at all: objects, places, people, movies, sounds, characters, and so on. Try to be as abstract as possible; move away from literal, rational connections, and focus on the feeling of the brand, not the product itself. This exercise can give you a sense for the messy mix of associations each brand harbors in our minds.

———————

The power of priming

You've probably heard of the sports and active wear brand, Puma. When you think of Puma, what comes to mind?

Maybe you imagine its sneakers, its clothing apparel, people you've seen wearing it, or ads you've seen from it. But, do you think of actual pumas (the great cats), or other cats? What about dogs? Probably not.

At least, not consciously.

Jonah Berger, a marketing professor and researcher at Wharton, did a study in 2008 with the great title, "Dogs on the Street, Pumas on Your Feet: How Cues in the Environment Influence Product Evaluation and Choice." In one part of the experiment, he exposed people to repeated images of dogs (not even cats!), and found that those who saw the dogs were significantly more likely to later recognize the Puma brand, and even feel more favorably toward it.[4]

Huh? People that saw images of dogs liked the Puma brand more? Yes. Exactly.

That, my friends, is the power of priming. Priming is the idea in psychology that when one stimulus is given, other associated words and ideas become more top-of-mind. For example, if you're given a list of words around a topic—say doctors—you're more likely to think of, recognize, and use words related to doctors, like "nurse."

There are a few other famous priming studies that have made it into the pop-science and pop-psychology worlds. Probably the most famous example of this is John Bargh's 1996 experiment that showed that people primed with elderly related words (for example, Florida, grey, retirement) would then walk more slowly than people primed with other kinds of words.

Another study showed that people who held a warm beverage in their hands rated their interviewer as more warm and friendly than people who held a cold beverage, presumably because the warm beverage primed them for the idea of warmth. The study I mentioned earlier—that showed when French or German music was played in a wine store it caused more of that country's wine to be purchased—is another example of priming at work.

My favorite example applied priming to brands. Professors Gavan Fitzsimons and Tanya Chartrand of Duke University, and Grainne Fitzsimons of the University of Waterloo, found in 2008 that very brief exposures to well-known brands can cause people to behave in ways that reflect traits of those brands. In the study, they exposed people to various stimuli at rates too fast to be processed consciously. Some of the participants briefly saw the Apple logo, whereas others saw the IBM logo. They were then presented with a creative problem-solving task: "List as many uses as you can for a brick."[5]

Amazingly, those who were exposed to the Apple logo generated significantly more uses for the brick than those who saw the IBM logo, despite having no conscious recollection of having seen either logo at all. The theory is that the Apple brand, and therefore its logo, has become so intertwined with the concept of creativity that even this brief 30 millisecond exposure to the logo caused people to actually act more creatively.

It is worth noting here that though these studies are regularly cited and have gained mainstream popularity, there has been some debate recently in the academic community around their validity. It seems many of the findings have proven difficult to replicate, particularly those that purport physical and behavioral changes due to priming. However, cognitive scientists widely agree that the basic idea of priming holds true, and that pre-exposure to one stimulus can implicitly influence us in various ways.

They also generally agree on what priming shows about how our memory works—that concepts in our mind are mentally linked together in a kind of vast network of associations. Just like "banana" and "yellow" share connections, or "doctor" and "nurse," "Florida" and "old," and "Apple" and "creative." In the case of Puma sneakers, dogs are related to cats, cats are related to pumas, and pumas are related to the sneaker brand.

Let's now take a closer look at these networks of associations, as they are another important piece for how Brand Fantasies exist in our minds.

Semantic networks: memory's web of associations

Without thinking about it too much, answer this question: what do cows drink?

What did you say? If "milk!" popped into your mind, and maybe is still sitting there, you're not alone. Think about it again. The ideas of "cows" and "drink" are both so closely connected to "milk" in our minds that it's hard to break out of it. But unless we are talking about baby cows, cows drink water, not milk.

This example illustrates another way in which our memory works. As psychologist Daniel Schacter and others have theorized, our memory for concepts seems to be linked together in what they call *semantic memory networks*. Semantic memory refers to all of the general knowledge about the world that we have accumulated throughout our lives. Things like cows are mammals, and the milk we drink comes from cows.

These ideas are then linked together in large mental networks of related ideas. So the idea of "cow" would likely be closely mentally connected to things like milk, beef, horses, farms, cheese, mammals, leather, grass, and on and on. Each of these individual concepts is a single node in the network, and each node has its own connections to its related concepts. It's a vast web of connected associations, kind of like the World Wide Web. There are lots of sites, and each site links to other related sites.

So not only are our memories biologically held in the brain as networks of connected neurons (or engrams), but they are also psychologically held as networks of associated connections.

The theory goes further to state that these ideas sit in a hierarchy of categories. So you may have a mental Animal category, and within that a category for Mammals, and Cows would sit in there. Connections that are more closely related

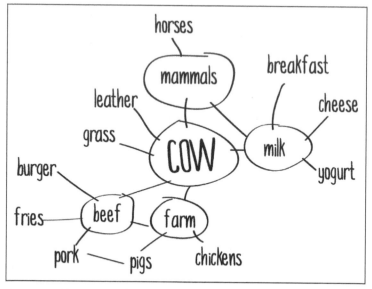

A semantic network example for the concept of "cow."

will be more easily primed, and will come to mind more quickly, will be stronger, and will last longer.

So when one concept is mentioned, it is said to be "activated," and this activation spreads outwardly from that point to other related concepts. It's just like watching waves ripple away from a stone tossed into a pond. This spreading activation among connected concepts explains why dogs were able to activate and prime the Puma brand, and why it's hard to not think "milk" when you hear "cows" and "drink." It's also why the Apple brand may make us more creative.

These networks aren't fixed or static. They dynamically evolve and change as we learn new things (again, just like how our neuronal connections grow and change). New information gets processed according to its related associations, and it can alter or strengthen existing connections. And these networks are very personal; they are based on individual experiences and personal beliefs. Your engram for Coca-Cola, Puma, or Apple will be slightly different from mine.

It makes sense that brands exist in this way in the mind. Our mind treats brands much like it treats anything else it encounters in life. Our brain perceives the brand, assigns meaning and emotion to it, and stores it in memory by connecting it to related concepts. A brand, therefore, is much more complex than the singular idea we assign to it in a simple positioning document—it represents an entire web of related associations.

Marketing then can be seen as the art of creating, managing, and developing these networks of associations in consumers' minds. We marketers are the spiders, spinning webs of connections that will form the representation of the brand in consumers' minds. This is how marketers create the Brand's Fantasy.

Brands are not singular concepts that exist as discrete items on their own in the mind. They are one node in a huge web of interconnected associations, ideas, feelings, and so on. Brands can activate other associations, but other associations (like dogs for Puma) can also activate brands.

Next, we will look at the important role of emotions in these associations and connections, and then see how they influence our decision-making.

Takeaways

- As we learn, our brain physically changes. Learning a new idea or skill means your brain's neural networks have been strengthened, altered, or created in some way.
- Memories exist as large networks of neuronal connections (called engrams) distributed throughout the brain.
- We reconstruct our memories each time we recall them. We put the pieces back together, and each reconstruction can be slightly different based on our current situation.
- Our memory is not as accurate as we'd like to believe and can be influenced by many factors.
- Not all memories are conscious. Implicit (unconscious) memories can stay with us and influence in subtle ways without us realizing it.
- Priming is an example of implicit memory in which one stimulus gets associated with something else, like the Apple brand and creativity.
- Semantic concepts exist in our minds as parts of networks of associations. When we activate or prime one part of the network, the activation

spreads outward across the network and related ideas become more top-of-mind.

- Similarly, brands live in the brain as part of huge, interconnected networks of related associations. Marketing works by building and managing these connected associations.

CHAPTER 4

Getting Emotional

The Real Role of Emotions in Branding

We are not thinking machines. We are feeling machines that think.

—Antonio Damasio

"We need to reach consumers *emotionally*."

If you're involved in any aspect of building brands, no doubt you've heard this, and phrases like it, countless times. The marketing world today obsesses over emotions. We want to elicit emotions, tap into emotions, uncover emotions, and understand emotions.

This wasn't always the case. Marketers used to focus on persuading consumers by touting their product's rational message and its functional benefits. You had to show and convince consumers why your product or service was better than the competition. Then the tides shifted. Today, any marketer worth his or her Morton's brand salt knows you have to romance and seduce your consumers with a carefully managed blend of rational and emotional messaging.

But what are emotions, really? And what does it mean to reach consumers "emotionally"? To quote Inigo Montoya from *The Princess Bride*, "You keep using that word, but I don't think it means what you think it means."

Emotions are messy things. They can mean lots of things, and mean different things to different people. Then you bring in related terms like feelings, attitudes, beliefs, and motivations, and who knows what we're even talking about anymore.

Through the past couple of decades, researchers have begun to build a much more complete view of how emotions work in our minds and bodies. In many ways, these new findings shatter what we previously thought—and what most of the public thinks—about emotions. Instead of being the opposite of rational thought, emotions are now seen as *integral* to rational thought. And instead of preventing calm, deliberate thinking, emotions actually *enable* it.

The marketing community today has only begun to scratch the surface of what emotions are, and how they can influence brand building and consumer decision making. As we will see, it's not about making consumers laugh or cry while watching your ads. It's not about telling them what emotion to feel, or even standing for an emotion, "owning" an emotion, or connecting a single emotion with your brand.

This is how we tend to think of emotions in marketing, which makes sense, because it's how we typically think of and talk about emotions in regular life. We see emotions as things you feel, like happiness, pride, inspiration, and so on. So we try to show these things in our marketing, imbue our brand with them, and connect with our consumers through them. But this is a too literal interpretation of emotions. It misses the role of emotions in influencing our behavior—the subtle and unconscious ways emotions can guide us and our decision-making.

In this chapter, I will try to help clarify what emotions are, show the amazing ways in which they influence us, and explain their potential role in building strong brands.

Emotions move us—literally

Remember our friend the sea squirt from Chapter 1? This little guy with the funny name is the creature that eats its own brain once it settles into a comfy spot, as it doesn't need to move for the rest of its life and, therefore, doesn't need its brain. The lesson: brains exist to help us move.

Brains exist to move us, and they do this by using emotions. We feel a certain way, so we do something about it. Emotions are motivators. In fact, the words "emotion" and "motivation" are cousins. They share the same Latin root, *movere*, meaning "to move."

So emotions may "move" us with feelings, but they also get us to move, quite literally.

Take the basic, universal emotions first described by Paul Eckman.[1] Anger gets you revved up and ready to fight. Disgust makes you avoid something potentially harmful. Happiness rewards you so that you repeat the behavior. Even sadness can cause you to stop, think, and reevaluate a situation. Evolutionarily, emotions helped us survive by getting us to *act*.

In today's world, emotions make less sense. We rarely, if ever, face immediate threats to our survival. But our evolutionary emotional wiring does still influence us today. We tend to act in ways that our emotions want us to. We can consciously override our feelings, but as you've probably experienced, it's hard to go against your heart. We trust our instincts and intuition, and rightfully so—they've kept us alive for millennia.

Emotions can even override our sensory systems. Take the bizarre Capgras syndrome, where patients can recognize faces, but believe that the people are "doubles," lookalikes that are impostors, not the real person. One theory for why this occurs is that though the person can see perfectly well and recognize the person as say, his or her mother, they have lost the feelings that connect with the perception. So although she *looks* like my mother, she doesn't *feel* like my mother, so she must be an impostor. They believe their feeling, even over what they see in front of their eyes. When in doubt, emotions trump all.

Do we cry because we are sad, or are we sad because we cry?

Let's say you're on a hike in the woods. Suddenly on the ground beside you, you notice something in the corner of your eye. You jump back, startled, unsure if it's a snake.

In that moment, your autonomic nervous system bursts into action. Your heart beats faster, your adrenal glands release adrenaline into your bloodstream, your muscles tense, your pupils dilate, and more. Your body prepared you for action, without any conscious thought or effort.

This illustrates two key points. First, emotions happen *to* us. We can't control them—they are evolutionarily hardwired to cause physical bodily changes that happen automatically. As organisms, we seek to create balance, or homeostasis. Our emotions help push and guide us toward behaviors and actions that should help maintain this balance.

The second thing it shows is that emotions happen in both the body and the mind. The great psychologist and philosopher William James famously wrote an article on the subject in 1884 called "What Is an Emotion?"[2] In it, he laid out his theory that emotions start as physical, bodily experiences that the brain then interprets and perceives as the emotion. In his example, if we see a bear in the woods, we might assume that we first feel fear, and then run because of that fear. He proposed it happens in the opposite order; we see the bear and automatically start running, then we feel fear. Our mind perceives our bodily changes, and then feels the feeling.

So it is possible that we feel fear because we tremble, and we feel sadness because we cry. Not the other way around.

This theory is now known as the James-Lange theory of emotion. Other theories of emotion claim we feel both the mental and physical aspect simultaneously, but one thing is clear: the brain and the body are tightly intertwined. Rather than being distinct silos, they work closely together, as our experience of emotions exemplify.

Antonio Damasio, one of the great neuroscientists of our time, takes this idea even further. He is a professor of neuroscience at the University of Southern California, and the head of the Brain and Creativity Institute. His recent book, *Self Comes to Mind*, posits the idea that consciousness and even our sense of selves—the "you" in your brain—comes out of the interaction of the brain and body.[3] He believes emotions that come from the body form the very foundation upon which our consciousness is built. Therefore, you cannot have consciousness without feelings.

To think, we must feel.

He even claims to have located where the sense of self exists in the brain. He says it must lie in the brainstem; the region of the brain that sits at the top of the spinal cord and base of the brain—the intersection between body and brain.

Damasio also distinguishes between "emotions" and "feelings," stating that emotions are the unconscious, physiological responses in your body, and feelings are the mental perceptions of those physiological changes. Emotions happen in the body, and then your brain and mind "feel" them, causing us to react. Emotions start as unconscious processes in the body; we only learn about them through feelings.

Damasio's influence on today's neuroscientific view on emotions, consciousness, and decision-making cannot be understated. His ambitious 1994 book, *Descartes' Error*, shed light onto the ideas that rationality and emotions weren't opposites, but actually worked together and required each other.[4]

The "error" in the title refers to what he believes was the philosopher Rene Descartes' error in separating the mind and body (this idea is often called Dualism), and separating rationality and emotions. To him, they are all closely intertwined.

Damasio's work demonstrates how unconscious emotions and feelings work with our conscious, rational mind to influence our behavior and the choices we make. So let's take a closer look at some of his hypotheses and work.

Trust your gut. You will anyway.

When we talk about "intuition," it often feels like a mystical, super-natural ability. We might have a vague sense for something, but can't quite put our finger on what it is, or how we've come to know it. It almost feels like a sixth sense. Other names for the phenomenon include "gut feelings," "gut instinct," or "having an inkling" about something. Women seem to be gifted with "women's intuition" which, at least in my experience, never seems to be wrong.

But what is really going on here? Though many believe it has something to do with spiritual energy in the air, or maybe connections to past lives, or some other paranormal activity, there is now scientific evidence that gut feelings are real and actually have a biological basis.

Take Damasio's most famous and seminal study, called the Iowa Gambling Task. In it, subjects were given four large decks of cards, two black and two red, and $2,000 worth of fake money. Each card tells the subject if they won or lost money, and by how much. The subjects, called "players," had a simple task: flip over cards from any deck, in any order, with the goal of winning as much money as they could.

Although the decks seemed to be random to the participants, in fact they were rigged. Two decks were "good decks" that had fewer penalties, but lower payouts (usually $50). The other two decks were "bad decks" that had higher risks, but higher rewards. It had very hefty penalties (over $1,000), but larger payouts ($100).

So the best strategy would be to pull cards only from the good decks, and avoid the bad decks. But the players didn't know the decks were rigged, and had no way to predict what kind of card they would pull.

In order to measure what was going on, the experimenters hooked up the players' palms to a machine that detects very subtle changes in electrical conductance of the skin. This is like a precursor to actual sweating (many of us get sweaty palms when nervous), and it reveals tiny flickers of emotion that are not available to the conscious mind. To get a read from the conscious mind, players were also asked occasionally what they thought was going on.

As it turns out, the conscious mind was slow to catch on. It took about 50 cards on average before players were able to discern that two decks were good and two were bad. Some players actually never figured it out, at least not consciously.

But their unconscious mind—their feelings—was way ahead of them.

After only about 10 cards, the respondents' palms began to sweat when reaching for cards in the bad decks. Somehow, their intuition was telling them to be nervous when choosing from those decks, as if they already expected a punishment. But when asked, they didn't yet consciously know any difference between the decks.

To prove the idea from another angle, they also did the test with neurological patients that had brain damage to the orbitofrontal cortex, an area involved in making decisions. These patients were terrible at the game, often losing all of their money. Though consciously they reacted similarly to the regular subjects, their skin never started to sweat, and they never had a feeling or hunch toward any of the decks.

Their brain damage prevented them from using their emotions to help guide their decisions, and so they were lost.

This also shows in their decision-making in real life. Many of these types of patients make terrible personal and financial decisions, and have trouble making ethical decisions. Without the help of their emotional drivers, they lose the ability to make sound decisions.

We humans are terrible at statistics and probability. Casinos take advantage of this fact every day, tricking us into thinking our odds are better than they are. But it seems evolution has given

Our brain unconsciously takes in and sorts all of the incoming data, and uses it to subtly guide our thinking and decision-making through the use of emotions. When we feel our gut is telling us something, or we have a hunch about something, it's our subconscious bubbling up and trying to send us a message.

us a trick to help us cope. Rather than needing to keep vast amounts of data in conscious memory and calculate what behavior would be better, our mind unconsciously takes in and sorts all of this data (through implicit learning, as we saw in the previous chapters), and then gives us a "gut feeling" or intuition as to what we should do.

Most of the time, these memories are covert. We don't know they are there, but they help guide us on an unconscious level from behind the scenes of consciousness. When they do make it into consciousness, we experience what we call a "gut feeling."

So gut feelings and intuition are how our unconscious emotions sneakily nudge us toward the better decision. We don't usually notice their input, but it's there. And more often than not, it seems, they are right.

Somatic markers help us decide

Being the good scientist that he is, Damasio created a more technical term for these gut feelings that influence our decision-making every day. He called them "somatic markers."

"Somatic" means relating to the body, and refers to the emotions that occur as bodily changes. These are the sweaty palms, elevated heart rate, tingling in our bellies, and other physical changes we feel in the body in connection with emotions.

By "marker," he means the feeling gets connected to some stimulus. In the Iowa Gambling Task, the bad decks were assigned a negative somatic marker, as shown by the sweaty skin response on the palms. In everyday life, as we implicitly learn about things we encounter, we assign markers to them, and then have positive or negative feelings for them. Positive somatic markers push us toward something, whereas negative somatic markers make us avoid things.

In the next chapter we will go further into how we make decisions, but for now, it is clear that our emotions help guide our actions. It is difficult for us to decide something if our emotions don't concur with it. You can override them consciously, but it takes effort. Think about times when you opted for a salad over the cheeseburger, or skipped dessert when presented with a decadent cake. In these moments you went against what your unconscious feelings wanted, but rationally knew was the smarter choice. So although we can make those kinds of choices at times, it's hard, and requires significant effort and willpower.

So emotions play a role in shaping our decisions for everything, including brands. Every touch point and interaction we have with a brand is like one more card being flipped over in the deck. We paint each brand experience with a positive or negative hue, so that each experience becomes another proof-point that our unconscious stores away and shapes our somatic marker, or gut feeling, toward that brand. And that will determine if we get excited, or if our palms begin to sweat, as we reach for it.

The truth behind "brand love"

Marketers today love to talk about building "brand love." We want to woo our consumers into a loyal, loving relationship.

We want them to only have eyes for us, and ignore the seductive calls from competitors.

And it's a worthy goal. Brands that achieve true love build fiercely loyal consumers. They will spend their own time and effort advocating on your behalf. They regularly engage with your brand. They won't dare give a flirting glance at the competition. They may even tattoo your brand name permanently (if somewhat sadly) somewhere on their body. And, of course, they create serious business value by driving volume and maintaining market share. We should all strive for such brand love.

But in reality, very few brands ever reach this state of marketing nirvana.

We can all probably think of at least a couple of brands that we'd personally say we *love*, that we stay loyal to, feel proud to own, and tell our friends about. For many people it's Apple, of course. Or perhaps it's their car brand of choice (I've seen passionate consumers of Lexus, Prius, Mini, BMW). Or maybe it's a brand in a hobby or passion you have, an article of clothing, a restaurant, or even an airline.

Then there's everything else. Everything that fills our grocery carts, our online shopping carts, and otherwise finds its way onto our credit card statement. We may actually be very loyal to many of these items or services; we may buy them monthly or weekly. We may never consider other options.

But how many of these things do we really *love*? How many would we go out of our way for? How many do we actively talk to friends about? Very few, if any.

The vast majority of brands don't get to be loved. They stay relegated to the friend zone.

These brands get picked up by *habit*. Most consumers can't, and don't want to, spend much time considering every purchase they make. So we trust our gut. We feel slightly positively or negatively toward it, so we buy it or we don't. Done. Decision made.

You might be thinking this only applies to quick, low-involvement categories, like gum, candy, or an app store purchase. It doesn't. Research shows that we tend to narrow down our choices even in super-high involvement categories—like buying a car or a house—to a set of options that we feel are possible contenders, and then choose from those. It's often our general gut feeling that gets those options put into the consideration set in the first place. The brand's somatic marker gives it a fighting chance to be considered.

True "brand love" is a dream very few brands will ever realize. Though it may sound less ambitious, building a strong Brand Fantasy for your brand—where the brand just feels right, and consumers have a positive somatic marker for it— is far more likely, and still very valuable in the marketplace.

So for most brands, rather than building a conscious feeling of "brand love," the best case scenario involves building a kind of unconscious, habitual brand loyalty.

To reiterate, building strong, conscious brand love is a valiant goal. If you work for a brand that has it, congratulations, and do everything you can to keep it. But I want to acknowledge the reality for most brands and most consumer interactions. Brand love is great, but getting to a place where your brand just "feels right" may be far more likely, and still highly valuable.

The good news is building a strong Brand Fantasy can do both. By shaping the unconscious associations with your brand, you first create the subconscious positive somatic marker toward your brand that gets you into the consideration set, and pulls the consumer to your brand. But it can also build the foundation for very strong conscious brand love as well.

So it's less about standing for an emotion or making your consumers feel an emotion with marketing, and more about guiding their unconscious feelings for your brand so that they feel positively toward it and are more likely to choose it over competitors. We'll describe how to do that in Part II.

Building somatic markers for brands

Brand somatic markers are not just built through advertising and other brand communications. They are built, piece by piece, every single time a consumer interacts with any part of your brand, even with your competition and related associations that don't involve your brand (remember dogs for Puma)!

So this has implications far beyond advertising. Everything will communicate: your design, distribution and placement, where your brand is mentioned, where your competitors are mentioned, how your brand appears in stores, who appears with it, the price, and on and on. Every sense is involved: the touch and feel, the smell, and the sounds all play a role.

Erik du Plessis, the author and chairman of market research firm Millward Brown, in his book *The Branded Mind*, coins the term "brand soma" for somatic markers for brands. For du Plessis, the brand soma encompasses the feeling of the brand. And it is the job of marketers to ensure the brand soma is strong and positive, and that advertisements, especially those in-store or at a point-of-purchase, effectively trigger the soma.[5]

He has applied Damasio's thinking about somatic markers to consumers' relationship with brands and advertising. I want to take it a step further in that not just advertising influences the brand soma, but also every interaction with anything even remotely related to your brand. The sum total of all of these associations forms the Brand Fantasy and the somatic marker for the brand.

Dr. Robert Heath writes in his book *Seducing the Subconscious* how "subconscious associative conditioning" is the method by which these associations get connected to brands.[6] You've probably heard of Pavlov's dogs—the famous experiment where Dr. Pavlov was able to have dogs salivate at the sound of a bell that they had come to associate with receiving food. After enough exposures to the bell, they were conditioned to the bell and would salivate when the bell rang, even without the food.

In much the same way, Heath argues that we consumers become conditioned to associations with brands. In his example, many of us still associate Michelin tires with their famous baby campaigns. The baby was a symbol of safety and to this day, many years after this campaign stopped running, Michelin is still highly associated with the baby and the idea of safety. He says it is *subconscious* conditioning because we don't know it's happening. These associations just wash over us as we go through our day without us realizing it, but can be very strong and long lasting.

The real story of emotions

In this chapter, I've tried to lay out a different way of thinking about emotions in building brands. Though most marketers agree we need to connect with consumers on an emotional level (rather than just a rational or functional level), there seems to be a lot of confusion around what this means. Rather than creating ads that make us laugh or bring us to tears (a very hot trend these days), I'm proposing we think about emotions more in terms of the general feeling consumers have toward a brand. This is how they relate to brands, and importantly, how they make purchasing decisions between brands.

Although it may be true that a great ad that tugs at the heart strings can get you more attention and engagement from consumers (and lots of buzz in the marketing industry), as we saw in Chapter 2, direct attention ain't all it's cracked up to be. As Heath argues, direct attention can cause counter-argument for your ads, and really, it's the subconscious associations that slip by and create the more powerful and long lasting effects on the brand soma.

So, maybe we should focus more on what those subconscious associations are, as they hold tremendous power in our purchasing decisions. The Brand Fantasy is a tool by which we can help understand, build, and shape those unconscious associations purposefully, rather than leaving them as an afterthought.

I hope this chapter shed light on what emotions really are, and the role they play in brands. In the next chapter, we'll apply this thinking to how we as humans make decisions in life, and for brands.

Takeaways

- Emotions aren't frivolous distractions; they are core to being human, and have helped us survive throughout evolution. Emotions exist to move us; they push us toward actions that will help us survive.
- Intuition and gut feelings are how our subconscious mind subtly influences us to choose options that should be advantageous. Our mind is constantly scanning and learning from the environment, and though that is far too much data to store and process consciously, our subconscious keeps track and pushes us toward the right answer.
- Damasio called these gut feelings "somatic markers." These are the general inclination or disinclination we have toward or away from something.

- When applied to brands, we see how every small encounter with a brand (or even things associated with it) influence our somatic marker for the brand and how we feel about it (also called "brand somas"). These then subtly but powerfully influence—in conjunction with our conscious minds—our purchasing decisions.

- This is very different from how most marketers think about emotions. Rather than being part of the conscious message (even emotional messages are conscious), the focus here is on shaping all of the subconscious associations with the brand to guide the Brand's Fantasy.

CHAPTER 5

Decisions, Decisions

The Truth Behind How Consumers Decide

I step up to the baseline. Across the net, the server bounces a fluffy tennis ball three times. Always three times. He tosses it up in the air, bends his knees, and explodes every muscle into the ball.

The yellow streak screams toward me at 120 miles per hour, reaching me in less than half a second. In that blink of time, I manage to turn, step toward the ball, and swing. I make contact, and I'm able (sometimes, anyway) to put a return back into play, all in less than a second.

During my junior and collegiate tennis career, this felt normal. But it should be impossible. How can the human body see, react, and execute precise movements that fast? How did I decide if I was going to hit a topspin backhand, or a slice? Down the line, or cross court?

How did I decide? I didn't. And that's why I could do it.

In a tight tennis match, thinking will kill you. You have to let go and let your finely tuned instincts, your intuition, and your feel drive you. The moment you try to take conscious control and think about each little decision you're making, the ball is already past you.

I've heard this from many high-level athletes in many sports. You need to trust your training and not think too much. For me, especially when I was playing well (or "in the zone" as athletes say), I would usually have a song running on endless repeat in my head. I would think of nothing but that song and let my body, almost zombie-like, play the match. I just tried not to get in the way.

Although most of us don't face 100-mile-per-hour serves on a regular basis, we do face many decisions every day as we go through life. And, usually, we don't spend too much time or effort deliberating every aspect of them. As we'll see in this chapter, our brains are lazy. We take the path of least resistance, and usually go with the solution that quickly and intuitively feels right.

In essence, we don't think our way through the world; we feel our way through it.

The illusion of rationality

We like to think of ourselves as rational, purposeful, and logical creatures. We feel like we make well-informed, deliberate decisions. Though it may be hard to believe, we now have decades of research that shows how our choices are often not optimal; our decisions are often influenced without our conscious knowledge, and we rarely make decisions when completely informed.

Despite this well-established knowledge, the rational illusion persists. We still want to believe we're fully in control, and our everyday experience seems to tell us we are, so it's difficult to believe otherwise. So we continue to market to consumers' rational and conscious minds and we continue to use market research that only asks the conscious mind what it can never know. Hopefully, this is beginning to change.

The Nobel prize-winning psychologists Amos Tversky and Daniel Kahneman helped bring this idea to light, starting in the 1970s. One of their studies asked people to estimate what percentage of African countries were members of the United Nations.[1] They wanted to see if they could influence subjects' guesses by exposing them to random numbers. They had respondents spin a wheel, "Wheel of Fortune" style, to generate a random number. They found that when the wheel stopped on a big number, the estimates for the number of countries in the UN suddenly increased. The subjects were obviously aware that this was a random number from a spin of a wheel, and has absolutely nothing to do with African countries or the UN, but still the number had a powerful influence over their guesses.

Dan Ariely, the behavioral economist who ran the vinegar beer study discussed earlier, ran another great study that showed a similar effect to that of Tversky and Kahneman. Ariely asked students to write down the last two digits of their Social Security number and then asked if they'd be willing to pay that amount for a bottle of wine. So if their last two digits were 52, they had to decide if they'd spend $52 on the bottle of wine. After they wrote down their answer, they were then asked to participate in a real auction—they could bid their own money for a few items (bottles of wine, chocolates, a book on design, electronics, and so on), and the winners would get to keep the items.

Writing down those two random digits before bidding shouldn't have any effect on their following bids, especially when their own real money was at stake. Rationally, it shouldn't, but as we now know, we're not rational.

It turns out, those random two digit numbers had a very strong effect on the students' eventual bids. The students whose Social Security numbers ended with 00–19 bid on average $67. The next group up, students with numbers from 20–39 offered an average of $102. This pattern continued through to the group with the highest random digits, 80–99, who bid on average $198, or *three times* as much as the lowest group, for the same exact items.

This is an example of the well-documented "anchoring" effect. And it's one example of many that show how we are not nearly as rational as we think. Ariely asked the students if they thought their Social Security numbers had influenced their bids, and of course they didn't think so. But as the numbers clearly showed, they had.

As Ariely writes in *Predictably Irrational*, "If I were to distill one main lesson from the research described in this book, it is that we are all pawns in a game whose forces we largely fail to comprehend."[2]

Many, many other studies show similar findings—that we can easily and predictably be influenced by things of which we have no conscious awareness. We saw this with Jonah Berger's priming study where exposure to dogs increased affinity toward the Puma brand, or when the music in the background affected buyers' choice of wines.

Now, we know we are not Spock from *Star Trek*. We're not cold, calculating machines that only do what makes rational sense. As many sci-fi movies have shown, we know that we're fleshy humans, with emotions and feelings that matter, even if they don't always make logical sense.

But we still like to believe that we make rational decisions in life. We think we know why we chose that car, or that insurance company, or the toothpaste, jeans, schools, politicians, and everything else we choose. But as the plethora of research shows, it's just not the case.

In fact, research with split brain patients shows just how much our conscious brain can try to justify our actions. Split brain patients have had their corpus callosum (the bridge between the two hemispheres of the brain) severed, meaning each side of their brains functions independently, without the normal communication from the other side. Some clever experiments have shown that when something is presented to only the right hemisphere and cause the patient to take an action, the left hemisphere, which had no knowledge of the input, will make up a story to justify the behavior.

For example, when one patient's right hemisphere was presented with the command to walk, he got up and started walking. When asked about this, his left hemisphere (the hemisphere that controls language and can speak, but didn't see the command), made up a justification that made sense and said, "I wanted to go get a Coke."

More often than not, our rational mind finds *justifications* for what our emotional brain wants. We chose that car because of the deal we got, because we liked the styling, or the miles-per-gallon, or the sunroof. But really, maybe we were just drawn to it, and those things helped us rationalize and justify why we liked it.

And maybe that's okay. Maybe we can accept that we are not cold and rational, and sometimes going with what feels right is just fine. If we get more pleasure out of it, maybe it is the right choice.

You still might be thinking that "this might be true for other people, but not me. I know why I buy my brand of deodorant." Maybe you noticed that the brand of deodorant works better for you than others you've tried. Maybe you like the smell. Maybe someone once told you that they liked the smell on you. But how did you try it in the first place? How did that brand make it into your set of options? Have you really tried all of the brands and focused on noticing the difference? Of course not.

Most likely, a few brands appealed to you, you tried them, and now you stick with what works. The key is how and why did it first appeal to you? How did that brand build a positive feeling that caused you to pick it up? There are probably many factors that contributed, most of which you never gave any conscious thought.

We like to think we are rational creatures, but clearly we are no such thing.

Who is really in control?

Not only are we not as rational as we think, we are also not as conscious as we think. Usually, when we're awake and sober, we feel fully conscious. We are in control of ourselves and our body. In general, we can do and think what we want.

But how much of this is an illusion?

Many neuroscientists believe that upward of 90 percent of what the brain does is not available to consciousness. If true, this would mean that we don't know what the vast majority

---

Think about something you recently purchased. Now try to work backward to what went into that purchasing decision. Ask yourself: How did I first learn about that product? Did I compare it to other similar options? What do I think drove me to pick up that one vs. the others?

Most importantly, how did my choice feel compared to the other options? What about that one felt better? What would it have felt like to have chosen one of the others?

Although it can be difficult to get a true read on your own behaviors, by looking into ourselves we can get a glimpse of what is really going on when our brains make decisions.

---

of our own brain is doing. This makes sense when you think about all of the actions our brain effortlessly performs without any conscious intervention. We don't walk around thinking about putting your left foot out, then the right, all the while focusing on balancing. We also don't think about the myriad of complex activities happening at all times simply to keep us alive: breathing in and out, keeping our heart beating, regulating temperature, digesting food, scanning our environment, and many, many more. Even if we tried, we'd have no idea how to work our own lymph nodes, release our own hormones, or get our immune system to attack a virus.

All of this happens to us, without consciousness, and without control. We're just the witness, an innocent bystander, watching it happen. So why then do we assume we're fully in control of the other more conscious parts of what the brain does?

Many thinkers have used the analogy of a computer and its monitor to represent our consciousness. Our brain is like the computer, working furiously behind the scenes and computing millions of bits of data every second. But then our conscious experience is like the computer's monitor. The computer only shows what is necessary for consciousness on the screen. We only consciously "see" what we have to for survival. We don't need or want access to all the back-end processing; we would drown in the overwhelming data, and be rendered incapable of doing anything. So the brain carefully curates what gets presented to consciousness.

This analogy also brings up another interesting point: the computer's monitor doesn't execute any actions. It doesn't decide. The computer does all the work and just displays its output to the monitor.

This would mean that our conscious mind is not actually executing as much of the actions and decisions as it would seem. Rather, it is merely responding to and executing the orders given to it by the deeper, emotional parts of the brain. Our conscious self is the observer, not the executor.

As the renowned neuroscientist Joseph LeDoux has stated, "The conscious brain may get all the attention, but consciousness is a small part of what the brain does, and it's a slave to everything that works beneath it."[3]

Researchers have even been able to predict a person's buying decisions based on their brain activity alone. In one study, subjects were put into an fMRI machine to view their brain activity, and asked to choose whether or not they wanted to buy certain items. By monitoring the activity in the nucleus

---

We're touching on the complex philosophical issue of free will. Are we really in control of our actions, or does our unconscious sit in the driver's seat, and our conscious selves are left seeing what happens and justifying it after the fact? There is no great answer to this question yet. Some philosophers believe we really have no free will at all, whereas others disagree. Some posit that consciousness plays the role of self-regulation—it's able to manage and control the unconscious drivers, at least some of the time. Whatever the answer, clearly there are many factors outside of our conscious awareness that influence our behavior.

---

accumbens (and other related areas of the limbic system), the researchers could predict—before the subject had even made a decision—whether or not the person would choose to buy. It seems the nucleus accumbens made the decision first, and then informed the higher order, conscious parts of the brain about its desires.

To be clear, I'm not saying we are complete zombies, at the mercy of our emotional wills. As Damasio and others have stressed, it is in the *interaction* between emotion and reason that the decision gets made. But it does seem emotions play a strong role in that decision, and that it's hard to override them.

One clever study showed just how hard it is to overcome our unconscious and emotional drivers. Baba Shiv, a researcher at Stanford University, divided students into two groups.[4] One group was asked to remember two digits, whereas the other group had to remember seven. They then had to walk down the hall to another room while holding their numbers in memory. In the other room, a researcher interrupted the students to ask if they wanted a snack, with a choice of sinful chocolate cake or wholesome fruit salad.

Interestingly, the students who had to remember the seven digits were twice as likely to choose the cake. The theory, according to Professor Shiv, is that the extra digits caused a greater "cognitive load" on the brain, and that this depleted the brain's willpower to make the "right" decision.

So it seems it takes actual physical energy and effort to override our desires. Willpower, in a way, is like a muscle with a finite amount of strength. If we tire it out, we're less likely to make the extra effort to override our emotional desires, and we give in. This is why we are often more likely to give in to temptation at the end of the day, when we're tired and can't put up a fight against our unconscious drives.

As anyone who has said they were going to eat healthy and then sees a dessert tray knows, sometimes what we consciously and rationally want to do (eat healthy) doesn't always jive with what our unconscious emotional drives tell us to do (eat the cake). Although we can override those drives some of the time, often we end up eating the cake.

Our lazy brains

The chocolate cake study makes another, more general point about the brain—it's lazy.

Compared to other organs in the body, the brain is greedy. It weighs only a few pounds, generally about 2 percent of our body weight, but it demands around 20 percent of our total energy needs. So for an average 2,000-calorie-per-day diet, 400 of those calories go to fueling your brain. As far as organs go, the brain is very expensive to operate.

But when you compare it to man-made machinery, the brain looks incredibly efficient. A typical adult brain runs on about 12 watts of power. That is just one fifth of the power needed to run a standard 60 watt light bulb. That's pretty impressive.

So how can this amazing piece of evolutionary machinery that constantly processes millions of bits of data with only 12 watts of power be considered lazy? Because the brain will do whatever it takes to find the easiest, simplest, and most effi-cient way to do what it does.

This means putting as much processing on "auto-pilot" as possible. As we have seen, we don't consciously think about most of what the brain does—how we process visual informa-tion from our eyes, or maintain homeostasis in our body. It just does them, without any conscious effort. This is true not just for physiological functions, but also for much of our decision-making through the use of mental shortcuts, called heuristics.

Heuristics: the art of shortcuts

Heuristics are mental shortcuts we use all the time to make decisions and judgments easily and efficiently. Think of them as "rules of thumb" that we use when there is just too much information to evaluate, and following the general rule will usually provide you with a good enough solution.

For example, if presented with jars of peanut butter, one with a familiar brand name and two with unknown brand names, most consumers will usually choose the one they know. This is the "familiarity heuristic" at work. When in doubt, choose what's familiar.

Another is the "availability heuristic," first coined by Kahneman and Tversky. This is when we assume something is important because it can easily and vividly be brought to mind. For example, when we're tempted to buy a lottery ticket, we can picture the news stories about recent lottery winners, but we don't think much about the millions who win nothing.

The experiment I described earlier in this chapter, where random social security numbers influenced people's bids, shows another heuristic: anchoring. We tend to use top-of-mind numbers as a starting point when choosing another number, even when the first number has no relevance at all to the choice.

One interesting heuristic that often goes wrong is the halo effect. This is when the positive or negative feelings we feel toward someone or something color our views about other aspects of them, even if we have no experience with it. For example, if we feel positively toward a person or brand, we tend to overlook their flaws. I have certainly seen this with many Apple devotees not noticing or acknowledging the many problems they have with their MacBooks.

Though heuristics are shortcuts, and purposefully exclude much of the possible information that could be taken into account, most of the time they work well. From an evolutionary standpoint, they had to. Our ancestors had to make quick decisions: Should I drink from this river? Should I fight with this person or flee? Should I try to make it back home or camp here? Rather than spend too much time or energy thinking through every scenario, outcome, and piece of data, we could fall back on these rules of thumb and make a quick decision based on a gut feeling that, most of the time, would be correct.

In fact, heuristics have been shown to rival deep statistical analysis at times. Criminal investigators, for example, will often use statistical modeling to help narrow down the location of a wanted criminal. They'll use tons of available data to weigh probable locations. But they found if they simply create a circle using the two farthest apart crime scenes, the criminal is very likely to be found near the center of that circle. This kindergarten-simple method, called the "circle heuristic," has been shown to actually be *more* accurate than the large quantitative data analyses.

So although heuristics can lead us astray—as shown by the many studies that prey on and exploit these tendencies—in normal life they tend to work pretty well. It's just like the assumptions our visual system makes usually work well, but these assumptions can be exploited and tricked by optical illusions.

Much of Daniel Kahneman's research has centered around the idea of heuristics, and the subtle ways in which they influence our decision-making. In his bestselling book from 2011, *Thinking, Fast and Slow,* Kahneman divides human thinking into two buckets, which he names System 1 (fast, automatic, unconscious) and System 2 (slow, conscious, deliberate thought).[5] These two systems are another way of describing how we are influenced by our gut feelings toward things, rather than conscious or rational deliberation. System 1 is a powerful influence on our behavior, even though we rarely notice it working. It happens in the background, shaping our thoughts and steering our actions. We can consciously override it, but as we've seen, our lazy brains usually do not want to put in the effort, and we'd rather go with what feels right.

The buying brain

Do I want whitening or brightening toothpaste? Are my teeth sensitive? Do I need baking soda, or Scope mouthwash in it? Do I care more about fighting plaque or gingivitis?

The toothpaste aisle boggles my mind. With only a couple of main brand players—Crest and Colgate—and then a handful of smaller brands, this category has exploded to rival the cereal aisle in terms of options. With the overabundance of choice running rampant in stores of all kinds, it's no wonder consumers easily get overwhelmed. And now with online shopping, and every version of everything accessible in a couple of clicks, the choices are endless.

Though having more choice may seem like a good thing, studies have shown that increasing the number of options can actually decrease the likelihood of purchasing anything at all, and that we'll actually enjoy our purchase more if we chose from fewer options. One study even found that speed daters had more matches when they met only eight potential partners than when they had gone through 20.

So the overwhelming choices out there hurt rather than help us find the best options. We don't want to, and really can't, evaluate all the options and make an informed choice anymore. So how do we decide?

For most of our purchases, we don't decide at all. The author Jack Trout found that about 85 percent of our purchases are habitual—meaning we just buy the same thing we've always bought without giving it a thought at all. I buy Colgate Total (I think), because I can't be bothered with all the others. And will it really make much of a difference? Probably not. I use the familiarity heuristic and just go with it.

So for marketers, a habitual purchase is great. It locks your product into a regular buying pattern, and builds repeated and expected volume. But how does a product become a habit and what about for high-involvement types of purchases that are only purchased rarely?

The classic purchasing funnel suggests consumers go through stages from Awareness, to Consideration, to Purchase, with different funnels having different variations on this basic theme. But this assumes a very conscious and rational approach to our purchases. As you've seen so far, it's the subconscious influences that matter as much or more than conscious consideration.

Let's look at a few examples. Say you're in a sporting goods store, shopping for workout T-shirts. There's a Nike section and an Under Armour section, both right next to each other (Dick's Sporting Goods stores are set up this way). Both sections have buff mannequins sporting the latest styles of sweat-wicking, technologically advanced T-shirts to sweat your guts out in. Both have racks of colors, sizes, and options, and the prices are evenly matched. Really, the products are nearly identical.

Even in terms of brands, they don't seem very different. You know, like, and respect both brands. You've seen both brands on top athletes, and maybe have even bought both brands before.

Assuming you're not interested in the other brands around the store, and are open to one of these two, what might pull you into the Under Armour section and not the Nike section, or vice versa?

To be clear, there is no clear-cut answer. Many, many things can affect this decision, and the science of decision-making can only go so far. You may have seen one brand more recently on your favorite football player. Or maybe a friend looked great in one of them. Maybe there's a sale on one, or they have one in your favorite color, or one display just pops out at you first. You might even try both on and see which fits and feels best. Who knows?

But, at some unconscious level, you probably have some deep-seated feelings toward each of these brands whether you realize it or not. You have a sense for what they're about, who they are for, and if they fit with your personal aspirations. Though probably none of that reaches your consciousness, it's still there, pulling some ropes behind the scenes.

In this case, maybe you've been wanting to try a new high-intensity workout class, and for some reason Under Armour seems the more appropriate choice for that. Maybe, to you, that brand feels a little more intense, has more of an edge, and seems slightly more at home flipping tires and doing hill sprints. That perception of the brand was probably built over many small interactions with the brand in the past, none of which you paid much, if any, attention to, and none of which you can recall now, but somehow they all add up to you putting an Under Armour shirt in your basket.

That slight feeling toward Under Armour, a gut feeling or "brand soma" that made that brand feel more right, made the difference. This is the Brand Fantasy at work—a collection of unconscious associations that slipped into your mind, mostly undetected, that guided your feelings for that brand.

This could be considered a medium-involvement purchase. It's not a huge investment that you will research a ton, but it's also probably not an impulse purchase that you just grab without a thought. Somewhere in between, you give it a few seconds worth of thought and just pick one.

Interestingly, this same process works for low and even high-involvement purchases as well.

For low involvement, it's probably a bit more obvious. Say you're in a checkout line, and happen to glance over at the vibrant display of candy bars and gums tempting you within arm's reach. You realize you need some gum, and grab a pack of Orbit ("Wintermint" flavor, because you want to live a little). You can see how this decision probably didn't get or warrant much conscious deliberation, and you probably just went with what felt right. Again, a "gut feel" guides you toward maybe a couple options, and you just pick one. No big deal.

But what about high-involvement purchases, like buying a car, a house, or even picking which college to attend? Surely, in these cases where large sums of money and possibly many years of your life are at stake warrant a more detailed, close inspection. But amazingly, even in these super high-involvement choices, people still tend to be guided by their gut and intuition.

Why else would real estate agents bake cookies when showing a home? If we humans had a shred of rationality, we shouldn't let the rich, warm, gooey smell of freshly baked chocolate chip cookies sway such an important decision like buying a home. Well, now I'm hungry, and this home is feeling really homey. Just like grandma used to make. Somehow, it feels more like home and I can just see us living a wonderful, fresh-baked life here.

Or take the car-buying process many of us dread. Out of all the cars out there, do we really research all of them, or most of them, or even half of the ones in the class and price range we are considering? More likely, you've had your eye on one in particular, or a few at most, and then maybe do your research, test drives, and haggling to narrow down from there. And even then, is it the specs that drive the decision, or is it the one you "just want" the most and can get the best deal on?

For many products, consumers will be happy with a very simple, one line point that justifies their choice. In spirits, maybe it's that this scotch was aged in port casks, or a whiskey filtered through maple charcoals, or a vodka that's distilled five times. These are nice, tidy, rational points you can use to feel good about why you bought that brand, even if they really had nothing to do with it.

——— —

As I hope you've seen, we're far less rational than we like to think we are. Evolution has built within us a system for making choices that is quick, efficient, and works well most of the

————————

*M*ore often than not, it seems our conscious mind plays the role of justifying the decision already made by our unconscious and emotional limbic system. We may tell ourselves we're buying something because we got a great deal on it, or because we love some specific aspect about it, but often the underlying reason we were drawn to it at all was the subconscious emotional feeling we had for it.

————————

time (and certainly worked well throughout evolution), but that can often lead us astray in today's world.

If we were rational, investors would always buy low and sell high (but often do the opposite). We would eat healthy. We'd save money for retirement. We wouldn't be swayed by a crossed out "list price" on something and think we're getting a deal. We would actually redeem mail-in rebates, and actually use gift cards (we tend not to do either). It wouldn't matter if we visit a potential university, or house we're thinking of buying, on a beautiful day or a rainy day. But it does. We're only human, and this is how we work.

We're guided by our gut feelings—Damasio's somatic markers—which are constantly being built and molded by our experiences. These intuitive feelings guide us through the world, with our conscious mind often as the observer and interpreter of what we've already decided to do.

Takeaways

- We like to think we are logical creatures, but as mountains of studies show, we are no such thing. We behave in irrational ways that often have evolutionary bases, but no longer serve us well in the modern world.

- Most of what happens in our brains is not available to consciousness. Our conscious mind is like the monitor of a computer—we just get to see the output, while most of the work happens behind the scenes.

- Our brains are lazy and will fall back on short-cuts, such as heuristics, for making decisions whenever possible. It takes effort to override our emotional desires and can be very difficult to do so.
- Much of our decision-making is driven by unconscious processes. We've been programmed by evolution to go with our feelings, for both low and high-involvement decisions.

———

Phew. That's the end of Part I, and with it, the end of the science-y chapters. If you haven't thought about the brain much before, I hope this section gave you a new appreciation for those three pounds of awesome behind your eyes.

I hope you've seen how so much of what we experience everyday doesn't reflect the reality of how the brain works. Because it's so different from what we typically experience, it can be hard to imagine that what we see is really more of our brain's interpretation of what's out there, or that we're unconsciously learning all the time, or that our memories are actually recreated each time we recall them, or that our emotions unconsciously guide us and our decisions.

Throughout these last chapters, I hope you've seen the importance of influencing the hidden and unconscious associations with your brand in consumers' minds, as those will be the more durable and highly influential associations when it comes time to purchase.

PART II

A New Model for Brands

Introduction to Part II
A New Model for Brands

Now that we've established a foundation for how the brain and mind work—especially the unconscious side of things—we can flesh out a practical model for how brands live in the mind.

As most existing brand models I've seen focus on the conscious side of brands, the goal of the Brand Fantasy is to bring the dark underbelly of brands—their unconscious associations—into the light. I want to bring these typically hidden and less-discussed parts of the brand on the table so that marketers can more easily work with and refine them for their brands.

My goal is to make the messy and nebulous world of unconscious brand associations more tangible and useful for anyone involved in building a brand.

Although marketers do understand the importance of a brand's equity, its personality, and tone of voice, I rarely, if ever, see these as a priority or focus of marketing effort and strategy. And really, even these elements do not capture the richness and depth of a Brand's Fantasy. They don't give you a real feel for the brand the way a consumer feels them. They're a good start, but we can do better.

Rather than feeling like yet another process that has to be followed, I hope creative marketers and agencies find this way of thinking liberating and, dare I say it, inspiring. But it's true. This model gives us the freedom to explore the deeper feelings of brands. It grants permission to focus more on the personality and mood we give to the brand, and frees us from the confines of strict conscious brand guardrails. It allows us to get messy, creative, and much like any artist, to go deeper into the feelings we want to create in our audience.

To me, this is the most interesting, exciting, and fun part of building brands, and I believe they are the key to unlocking brand growth and value.

In Chapter 6, we'll begin by looking at why we need a new model for brands at all, and what is missing in the current systems. Chapter 7 will then provide the tools to build your own Brand Fantasies for your brands. Then, in Chapter 8, we'll look at the Brand Fantasy in action with a few case studies.

Let's give the forgotten side of brands their due.

Capturing Cool

Why We Need a New Way of Thinking About Brands

In business, being cool matters.

I don't necessarily mean "cool" in "The Fonz" kind of way. Or even in the Justin Timberlake, Tom Brady, or Lady Gaga kinds of ways. I mean having a style and image to your brand that your customers aspire toward. This is true regardless of the industry or category, B2C or B2B, or age and demographics of your target. Anything can have its own kind of cool. Anything.

Virgin and JetBlue made airlines cool. GEICO is arguably some kind of cool within insurance. Sunglasses were always cool, but Warby Parker made buying plain old eyeglasses cool. Startups like Casper and Tuft & Needle are making shopping for mattresses cool. If mattress buying can be cool, anything can be. Even the most corporate, business-to-business products and services—look at Dropbox and Box.com—can have a sense of style that causes their customers to choose them over the competition. Business people are still people, after all.

Whatever the industry, people will choose your product or service (assuming the product itself meets their needs), because it embodies something they want to be a part of. It has the kind of cool they want from that category. So cool can take many different forms; the key is to find *your kind of cool*, and do everything you can to build and maintain it.

Of course, anyone who tries to be cool isn't. We can smell inauthenticity a mile away. You have to start with what's already in your brand's DNA, and build from there. Any brand will have something about them, some nugget deep within, that they can build a story around that imbues their brand with the feelings their target aspires to.

The problem is the tools we have for managing brands today largely ignore what makes a brand cool.

The Brand Fantasy model tries to capture a brand's unique coolness, and put it into a tangible format that can be worked with, discussed, and used to guide everything a brand does. I say "tries" because that is no easy task. How can you capture the feeling of what makes something cool? It's not easy, and this model is not perfect, but we should try our best, because it is in these feelings—the style, image, mood, and attitudes—associated with brands that breed loyalty and create strong brands. As we saw in Part I, it is in these unconscious associations that we form our opinions about brands and that drive our decisions.

It's much easier to talk about a brand's conscious aspects, its functional and emotional benefits. Maybe that's why marketers have clung to them for so long. But if we're in the business of making brands cool, we should at least aspire to having tools and language that lets us do so.

Admitting we have a problem

If you work in marketing for a medium to large corporation, or for an agency that works with big brands, you've likely come across their way of capturing what their brands are about. Usually, these take the form of some kind of one-page document that encapsulates the key elements of the brand, with the goal of ensuring all consumer touch points stay true to this definition of the brand. I mentioned these kinds of brand models earlier, but I'd like to take a closer look here as it will help set up where we are going.

I've seen brand architectures, brand onions, brand temples, brand wheels, brand pyramids, many forms of overlapping circles, and others. Although the format changes, you typically see some combination of these elements:

- **Product Attributes:** Description of what the product is, defining features, brand heritage, design elements, and so on.
- **Functional Benefit:** What the product does, functionally.
- **Emotional Benefit:** The larger emotional benefit felt by consumers.
- **Marketplace/Competitive insights:** What the competitive environment looks like, and how this product is different.

- **Cultural Insight:** What is going on in culture that this brand can tap into.
- **Target Description:** A short description of the target market, including both demographics and "psychographics."
- **Target Insight:** A truth about the consumer that the brand can tap into.
- **Tension/Enemy/Conflict:** A negative or opposing force in culture or within the target's mindset for which the brand offers a solution.
- **Highest Ground/Vision/Mantra/One Word Equity/Purpose/Core:** A short, pithy word or statement that captures the brand's core belief, value, or reason for being. This is the big, over-arching idea.
- **Personality/Tonality/Archetype:** Description of the look and feel, tone of voice, and personality of the brand.

These are all important in building a strong brand. You do need to know who your target is, what cultural trends you fit in with, how you're different from your competition, the values of your consumer, and how your brand can align with them.

But I have two issues with these types of models: 1) They focus almost exclusively on the conscious side of brands and 2) They make brands feel one-dimensional. Let's look at both of these issues.

Even the more emotional aspects—emotional benefits and target insights—tend to relate more to conscious emotions. For example, Tide might say that, for moms, its brand is part of being a good parent and a way they show their love is by taking care of their families. That may be indirect, not top-of-mind, and it certainly is emotional, but it's still a conscious aspect of the brand. The consumers may not think about it all the time, but you can easily get them there through some basic questioning and probing. They think of Tide as cleaning their clothes, which in turn makes them feel good as a parent and caretaker of the family. So though it is less top-of-mind, it's still there, available to consciousness.

That doesn't mean it's not important. By standing for those values of being a good parent and taking care of your family, Tide can align its brands with parents who share those values. That can be one more piece that makes consumers feel positively toward the brand.

The problem is it's only half the battle.

Unconscious associations that come from things like the vibrant colors of the Tide package, the name "Tide" which cues waves crashing against a rocky shoreline and feels clean and fresh, and maybe that you've seen it on your mom's shelf growing up, all give the brand a strong feel that can pull consumers in. Those things may seem peripheral and secondary, but they're not. They should be considered central to the brand.

The one piece of these models that does touch on the unconscious feel of the brand is the lowly "brand personality" or "tone of voice." This often-ignored piece of the puzzle tends to sit in some forgotten corner of the document, relegated to an after-thought. We assume the brand's look, feel, and tonality can't matter that much. And anyway, we assume, the agencies and designers will figure that out. More often than not, brand personalities come down to an "I'll know it when I see it" mentality. There is an opportunity to be much smarter about it.

Even when we connect our brand to strong emotional desires or deeply held brand values, we're still falling into the conscious trap. We're assuming consumers will consciously hear and comprehend our emotional message (a message that is often at least a step or two removed from the actual product), remember it, connect it with our brand, and then use that knowledge to choose our brand over the competition. But as we saw throughout Part I, this is not how we humans work. It's how we like to think we work, and maybe how we'd want to work in an ideal world, but it's not how we actually work in this world.

My second point of contention with these models is that they make brands feel very one-dimensional. Like a supporting character in a bad sitcom, we box the brand into one thing,

---

*M*any brands use the idea of archetypes to help describe the character of their brands. I like the idea of archetypes in theory—they attempt to capture the essence and character of the brand—but in practice, I find they are often trivialized. It can feel silly to think of your brand as an "Outlaw," "Creator," or "Magician" (and what do those even mean?). In my experience, agencies and marketers tend to choose one to check the box, and then quickly ignore them.

---

where it gets to be only that thing and nothing else. We marketers want things to be simple, clean, and concise—"single-minded," as marketers like to say. But in reality, we relate to brands in a more complex, nuanced, messy, and abstract way.

The value of the brand, not just the devil, is in those details.

No matter the brand or category, we relate to things in our environment with a nuanced mix of abstract feelings and associations. Everything is multi-dimensional. Even your toilet paper brand, which you may not want to think too much about, will have a complex network of associations in your mind built through the years of experiencing the product, the name, the design, the ads, the price, where you've seen it, and so on.

A brand may stand for one thing functionally (for example, Charmin is toilet paper and closely related products like wipes, but can't be much else), and it may have a single strong belief and point of view (for example, Volvo owns the idea of "safety"). But to say the brand is *only* about that one thing is to do it a disservice. When we do that, we lose much of what gives the brand a personality, feeling, and soul that consumers can connect with.

In order to capture those more subtle elements, we need a new method of talking about brands, and even a new language.

Do you speak "mentalese?"

What is the language of thought? Do our thoughts come to us in fully formed sentences, in fragments of ideas, symbolic images, or something else? Can we even comprehend our own thoughts, using our thoughts?

Renowned MIT cognitive scientist and linguist Steven Pinker coined the term "mentalese" to describe a hypothetical language of thought. In his theory, mentalese is the way concepts are represented in the brain, including the meaning of words. He believes these happen in a more symbolic and conceptual way, before they can be represented by language. So although we may consciously think in our native language, there is a lot of other thinking and processing going on that takes place without language.

In a way, language is our crude instrument that allows us to translate mentalese into something we can share with another person. We try to build the mental image we have in our head in the listener's head through language. But many cognitive scientists believe that language is a poor way of doing this, and we lose a lot of what makes up an idea in the mind when we force it into the rules of language.

This can be a hard concept to grasp—it's hard to think about the nature of thinking. But the point is that much of our thinking likely happens in a very messy, symbolic, and conceptual way, rather than in clear and distinct sentences. And, most likely, this is the way brands are represented in our minds and our subconscious.

Daniel Dennett, a preeminent philosopher and cognitive scientist (who looks exactly as you'd hope a philosopher would look—long white beard, glasses, elbow-patched blazers) wrote a book on the topic in 1991 called *Consciousness Explained*.[1] As the title audaciously states, Dennett describes his theories for how the brain creates consciousness, centered around his now famous "Multiple Drafts Theory."

To oversimplify this theory, he believes consciousness doesn't live in any particular place in the brain, but rather arises out of the connections and myriad processes happening in the brain. He sees the brain as a kind of "echo-chamber," where many thoughts and ideas are bouncing around, and only those that reach a certain level of activation will reach conscious awareness. It's a kind of "parallel pandemonium" where many thoughts and processes are happening subconsciously.

It's not a huge leap that when we think of brands, we don't just think of one clean positioning statement, or a single-minded brand point of view. Rather, we have a whole mess of related thoughts, ideas, and feelings swimming around in the mind associated with the brand, most of which we don't consciously register, but may be exerting powerful subconscious effects behind the scenes.

So if brands live in the mind in "mentalese," and in a parallel pandemonium of "multiple drafts," shouldn't our brand documents also reflect that (at least as close as we can get)?

But no, we *translate* brands from this messy and symbolic mental language into neat and tidy brand documents, with clear sentences and checked boxes. We translate them into our normal language of life and business. We make them simple and clean, but in the process, we lose the essence of the brand. We lose the feeling of the brand. We lose its soul.

A lot gets lost in translation.

I believe we relate to brands like we relate to people. We have a mix of experiences and interactions with someone, and they all add up to a feeling we have for that person. Think about someone you know well—could you ever really capture your feelings for them in a brand pyramid? You may be able to capture certain aspects of the person, but the nuance and subtleties, the mix of emotions and thoughts, and just the feeling of the person would be lost.

So if we want to capture the essence of a brand, we should do it in a way that tries to capture the feeling of a brand. In fact, the model itself should be felt more than stated.

Emotional confusion

As discussed earlier, there is a deep-seated myth lurking in the halls of marketing today: the misunderstanding of the role of emotions in building brands. It has become very popular to talk about how consumers make choices emotionally, and relate to brands emotionally. As we have seen, there is certainly a lot of truth to that, but the misunderstanding comes in how we execute against it.

Currently, there seems to be two routes we take to connect emotionally with consumers (with a lot of overlap between them):

1. We try to stand for or "own" an emotion or value (like trust, freedom, nurturing, goodness, and happiness).
2. We build communications that try to elicit emotions out of us (as seen in the trend of tear-jerker TV ads and digital films in the past few years).

Both of these try to hit on emotions directly, overtly. And they can work. They can help align your brand consciously with the values of your consumers. They can also create strong unconscious emotional associations with your brand that can help make it more likely to be purchased.

But they are not the only ways to do it.

I believe you can have great marketing and communications that build strong associations for your brand, without ever being so overt about the emotions you are trying to elicit. Apple rarely talks overtly about being more creative, stylish, or in-the-know. They are just built that way, and act that way in everything they do, from the design of their products, to their stores, packaging, and people. They exude creativity and coolness, without the need to say it.

Instead of needing to hit emotions head on, we should realize that the emotion that matters for purchasing decisions is the somatic marker, the feeling you have for the brand in general. It's the sum total of all those tiny associations with the brand. This feeling can be built in any number of ways. Standing for emotions and eliciting them with your communications is one way, and can be very powerful associations to build, but it is not required and actually may not be the best way.

Building a better model

I hope by now you're feeling that there's a lot of room for improvement in how marketers think and talk about brands. For too long we've clung to the conscious illusion. Despite the constant talk about how consumers are driven by emotions, or by unconscious influences, we still build conscious-focused brands, ignoring the deep, dark underbelly of unconscious associations.

It's time to change. It's time we embrace the unconscious mind of the consumer in all its scariness, messiness, and irrationality. It's time we started to work with the reality of how brands exist in the mind, rather than the illusion we've built for ourselves on how we'd like them to exist.

The burgeoning field of neuromarketing has begun to lay a groundwork for bringing neuroscience thinking to marketing. They have opened the eyes of marketers to how much we can learn by peering into the brain, rather than by asking the conscious mind. However, neuromarketing today seems mostly limited to the testing of ads, websites, landing pages, or package design, for example. It is involved mainly at the *end* of the creative process, when communications and consumer-facing materials are already developed.

I'd like to flip that. Rather than being an end-point (that many creatives say kills creativity), let's move neuroscience understanding to the front of the process to inspire better brands and marketing. The smarter we get about how brands work in the mind, the more we can create brands that truly connect with consumers and differentiate themselves in the marketplace. We can ask smarter questions and build smarter brands. I find that inspiring and exciting, and I hope you do too.

Takeaways

- Every brand should find its form of "cool"—a style, image, and attitude that its consumers aspire toward and want to connect with. This is true for any brand in any category, including B2B. Current brand models fail to capture the coolness of a brand.
- Brand models tend to focus almost exclusively on conscious aspects of brands, even when talking about the emotional benefits of the brand. Though these pieces are important, we must also consider the unconscious side of brands, as they can have as great or greater impact on the brand's value.
- Top cognitive scientists believe that ideas, and therefore brands, exist in the mind in a mental language called "mentalese" and in concurrent "multiple drafts." Our brand models should reflect this as closely as possible, because it more closely matches the reality of how brands live in the mind.
- Though marketers today know the importance of connecting with consumers "emotionally," there seems to be a lot of confusion around what that means and how to do it. Currently, the idea of building a brand's somatic marker, or general feeling for a brand, is not part of the "emotional" conversation.

- The goal of the Brand Fantasy model is to create a way of working with the unconscious associations with brands, as they are crucial to building a strong brand. It's a tangible tool to help us decode our messy, abstract, and nuanced relationship with brands.

CHAPTER 7

The Brand Fantasy Model

Making the Intangible (Somewhat) Tangible

After all this theoretical talk, you're probably ready for some practical applications of this thinking. In this chapter, I'll lay out my suggestions for how to start working with the unconscious network of associations with your brand, what I'm calling the Brand Fantasy. We'll dig into a suggested model for how to make this nebulous, intangible idea at least somewhat tangible.

Let's acknowledge from the outset that it won't be easy. The Brand Fantasy is messy and abstract. It's a constellation of interconnected associations, feelings, moods, attitudes— not easy things to capture on paper. On top of that, we all have slightly different associations with a brand, and different ways of wording and imagining them. It's not perfect, but we should try.

If you've taken anything from this book so far, I hope it's that the unconscious side of brands is as important, if not more so, than the conscious side we spend so much of our time and effort building. Our unconscious beliefs, perceptions, and emotions guide how we move through this world, and how we make decisions. As we saw in the last chapter, our current brand models are woefully incomplete, ignoring this ocean of important brand associations.

This doesn't have to be a whole new way of working. It should work alongside and complement the tools you already have. You can let your existing tools manage the conscious side of the brands, and then add this to represent and capture the abstract unconscious side.

This is not a strict set of guidelines. I believe the model should be flexible and allow your Brand's Fantasy to shine through in whatever form works best for the particular brand and for your organization. The point is to capture and

---

*T*he purpose of using the Brand Fantasy is to create a shared language and understanding that helps us guide and build the brand toward a common goal. It gives everyone who touches the brand (not just the marketers!) clear direction, guardrails, and a filter for what we want this brand to feel like, and what we do and don't want associated with it. It provides a North Star to build toward.

---

communicate the associations and feelings connected to your brand, not to check boxes.

So use these items as suggestions only, and feel free to get creative with it. It can be adjusted and molded depending on the brand and your needs. We shouldn't force-fit the brand into the model; we should shape the model around the brand.

The goal is to capture your brand's version of cool. It's the aura of your brand, the feeling you want your consumers to have when they think of it. To do this, we will need to let go of the logic and order we're used to in business settings. We should embrace the mindset of an artist: be open to exploring different concepts, techniques, and imagery with the goal of capturing an elusive and nebulous feeling.

We need to embrace the messiness.

Building a network of associations

As we saw in Part I, our memory exists, both at the biological and cognitive levels, in networks. It seems memories are physically stored in the brain through vast networks of neuronal connections (engrams), and similarly, concepts exist as parts of large interconnected networks of associations. Remember, the brand Puma has associations with cats, which are associated with dogs. Brands exist as one node in this complex web of associations, with many other concepts attached to it.

Because brands live in the mind as a network, we'll build our model as a network. Remember, our goal is to more closely represent how brands actually live in the mind, rather than how we'd like them to live on tidy sheets of paper. We'll try to show what some of the brand's related associations might be, and what we'd like them to be. The key is to build an overall mental image and feeling of the brand.

If you've ever worked with a "mind map," this will feel familiar. In mind mapping exercises, you write down one concept, say "weight loss," and then write related ideas around it, with lines connecting them. So if in the center of the page you have "weight loss," related ideas might include "exercise," "eating well," "Weight Watchers," "diet fads," "calories," and so on. Then you can expand from there by circling one of them, say "exercise," and create a list of related words that are connected to exercise, like weight-lifting, running, yoga, and so on. As you build your way outward, you create a networked map of interrelated ideas. We'll use this technique to represent the associations connected to your brand.

And rather than provide a strict template to fill out, I'd like to give you a few suggested pieces, and let you bring them to life in whatever way suits your brand, company, and style.

Meet your brand, as if for the first time

You might think you know your brand or brands really well. Maybe you work on them all day, every day. Maybe you're even a passionate consumer of them yourself. It's great to have a comprehensive knowledge of your brand's conscious aspects, and that will make this process easier, but have you ever really stopped to focus on the underlying *feel* of the brand? Have you ever really explored the deeper connections and associations with your brand that may not be conscious? If you're like most marketers I know, you probably haven't.

Before we can begin compiling the different associations, we need to feel the brand for ourselves. We need to intimately know, from the inside out, the soul of our brand. We have to experience it for ourselves before we can try to capture it.

Tapping into the unconscious ain't easy. By definition, it's not available to the conscious mind, and philosophers and neuroscientists have long debated whether or not introspection (looking within your own mind) can ever give us a real view into what's going on. Can the brain use itself to understand itself? Did your head explode yet?

This is not just where the brand is today, it's where you want the brand to go. It should be aspirational; it's what you want the brand to feel like in consumers' minds and hearts once you've nailed it with all your marketing efforts. So dream big, and make this the ideal place you want your brand to eventually reach.

To tap into our own unconscious feelings of the brand, we'll need to use a few techniques. These will be similar to some of the projective market research techniques we'll discuss later, which makes sense, because those are how you can bring out the same unconscious feelings from your consumers. Here, we'll use them on ourselves to tap into our feelings about the brand.

Remember, we will be translating these feelings from the mental language of "mentalese" into something more tangible. So yes, something will likely be lost in translation, but it's the best we can do.

Probing your unconscious

Before we can attempt to access these subconscious feelings and associations in your mind, we'll need to break out of our business-as-usual mindset. We have to let go of the usual clear cut rules and the desire for well-defined ideas.

To do that, I suggest kicking it off with a mini self-hypnosis or meditation style session (this might sound a little crazy, but stay with me). Find a spot where no one will bother you, sit in a comfortable chair, and let's really get into it. Clear your mind, silence your phone, and let go of the daily worries and constraints. (If you're hesitant about this, I don't blame you, but I just ask that you give it a real shot.) Give yourself just 10 minutes of uninterrupted focus time and the freedom to dive into the depths of your brand. It's amazing what an uncluttered and free mind can do in just 10 minutes.

If you have a physical product, keep it nearby for inspiration. If not, look at your logo, website, app, or any other materials that can bring your products, services, and brand top-of-mind. Remind yourself of your customer's experience and try to get into their mindset when interacting with your brand.

Then take a few deep breaths, relax, and close your eyes. Let your imagination wander in, out, and around your brand.

Think about this simple question: "What does [Brand X] feel like?" For example, is it clean, fresh, and bright? Is it rugged, burly, and western? Is it warm, fuzzy, and cuddly? Is it sleek and minimalist?

Force yourself away from the literal. This isn't about what the product itself physically looks, feels, or tastes like. It goes beyond the corporeal product that exists in the physical (or digital) world. For the purposes of this exercise, you'll want to divorce the product and brand—think of them as two distinct things. We'll bring the product back in later, to be sure, but for now, it's helpful to break away from the confines of the product and delve into the ethereal brand. It's the soul living within your product, the brand ghost in your product machine.

Also, don't fall into the trap of typical personas, characters/archetypes, or clichés that you already know. Your brand can feel like anything and in fact shouldn't be a direct copy of other things out there (this is one of my issues with relying too heavily on "archetype" descriptions—they limit you to a set list of existing clichés).

I realize this can sound strange and can be a bit tricky, so I suggest trying a few thought experiments that can help guide your thinking. You can mix and match these, and try whichever ones work best to capture your brand's unique underlying feelings.

- **Go through every sense:** What does your brand look like; what imagery comes to mind? What does it sound, smell, and taste like?

How does it feel to the touch? Is it warm and fluffy? Sharp? Rough? What else could it be? (Remember, this is not the literal look, taste, or feel of your product, but rather what the *brand* would look, feel, or taste like.)

- **Create a brand world:** Imagine your brand has its own little planet, *Star Wars* style. What would life be like on this planet? What are the climate, terrain, and weather like? Who would be there, what would they be wearing, driving, and doing?

- **Create a brand persona:** If your brand was a person, who would it be? Paint as detailed a picture of the person as you can. Think about: is it male or female, its age, what would he/she wear and do for a living, what kind of car would he/she drive, what would he/she do for fun, what kind of food would he/she like, who else would they hang out with, and so on.

- **Throw a brand party:** If this brand threw a themed party, what would it be like? Where would it be, who would be there, what would be served, what kind of music would be playing, what would the atmosphere or vibe be like, and what activities would be going on?

- **Take the brand away:** Imagine the world without this brand. What would be missing? How would things feel differently? What would people do instead, and how would that be different?

- **Explore other metaphors:** Open your mind to think of anything else that relates to your brand's feeling. This can be almost anything that captures a hint or taste of your Brand's Fantasy. Maybe a particular movie, TV character, or a celebrity captures an aspect of your brand. Maybe a song or musician, or something about a certain car, household object, fabric, food, or something else feels like a part of your brand. Or maybe a work of art or poetry captures part of your brand's feeling. There are no wrong answers and almost anything can work.

Try a few of these and pick whichever works best for your brand. If you feel like one of them gives you a clear mental image, go with that.

Once you feel like you have a good sense for the feeling of the brand, hold on to it! Keep it in memory. A good idea is to pick one thing that helps *trigger* that feeling so you can recall it—maybe an image, a smell, a song, a movie, or a character. Pick something that worked particularly well, that when you thought of it you said, "Yes! That's it!" Keep that in mind so we can then build the Brand Fantasy around that feeling.

Making it real

Now that you have your brand's feeling in mind, it's time to make it tangible. We'll try to capture the richness of those feelings you elicited onto paper, so that it can be shared, used, and worked with. The point is simply that you capture your brand's feeling in a way that can be understood by anyone that touches the brand, and in a way that inspires creative marketing and branding materials.

Here are four main elements I like to use for capturing and piecing together a Brand's Fantasy, but remember these are just suggestions:

- **Core words:** A list of 3–5 words that together begin to capture the feeling, fantasy, and essence of the brand.
- **Fantasy network:** The largest piece, this is the "mind map" that lays out the network of key associations with your brand.
- **Multidimensional mood board:** An abstract representation that goes beyond the limitations of language and brings the Fantasy to life with images and metaphors.
- **Trigger:** A single word or short phrase that functions as a shorthand or symbol for the rest of the full, rich Fantasy.

Let's look at each of these in a bit more detail.

Core words

I like to start by listing words that capture the essence of the brand. Make a long list at first—free associate and capture all the concepts that come to mind related to that feeling. Go for quantity; you can narrow down later.

Once you have a good list, read back through it and identify your favorites. Mark the ones that really nail at least a certain aspect of the Brand's Fantasy. Keep filtering and culling until you have those top few words (3–5 usually works) that when placed together bring up the feeling in your mind, at least in part. Think of these words as a team, where each one plays a complementary role to the others. So rather than having synonyms, each word should represent one distinct aspect of the brand. If you have similar words, pick the one that fits the best.

The goal of these words is to have a shorthand that can easily and quickly bring up the Brand's Fantasy. They cue it, without having to go into too much detail. They should also be pretty telegraphic, where someone with little knowledge of the brand can get the gist of it just from those words.

The fantasy network

Here's the meat of it—building out the fantasy network. This is where we try to replicate and put onto paper something similar to the network of connections and associations in your consumers' minds related to your brand.

Look back at the longer list of words you made for the core words and see if you can cluster these into groups. A good way to do this is to put each word, phrase, or idea onto a Post-it note so they can be arranged easily on a wall. You'll probably start to see a few groups emerge as they coalesce around a few key themes or ideas. This is more of an art than a science, so go with what feels best and captures the feeling you had in the meditation exercise.

It seems having about three to five of these groupings works well, as it's enough to give the brand depth, dimension, and richness, but not too many to be overwhelming. Once you have a few groups, give each one a name that captures the main idea of that group. (These can be the same as your core words, but don't have to be.) Then choose a few of the key phrases or ideas within the group to flesh it out beyond just the title.

I like to think of each of these groupings as an individual "planet" that "orbits" the main idea. Eventually, once you've laid out all of your planets and their corresponding associations, you can actually draw this up like a little solar system. You'll have the trigger in the center, followed closely by the core words in the next concentric circle out. You'll then have these 3–5 planets orbiting that central nucleus. Together, these give you a sense for the main feeling of the brand in the center and its network of associations as you expand outward.

In fact, if you've done this well (and already have a well defined brand to work with), people should be able to tell what brand you are talking about just by showing them this mind map, with no mention of the brand name, product, or category on the page!

This simple one-pager can give you a good sense for the Brand's Fantasy and underlying, unconscious feelings, but it has a key limitation: it uses only words. Words are our crude instruments that attempt to capture the ideas in our minds and feelings in our bodies, but they rarely get the whole thing. Our language is no match for "mentalese."

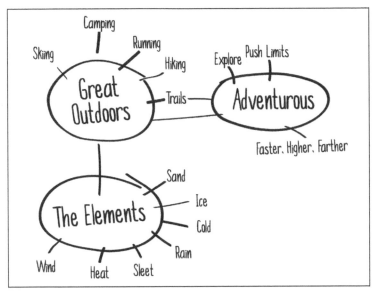

Can you guess what brand this fantasy network might be for? (I was thinking The North Face).

So to add to our mind map network and better represent the feeling of the brand, we need to go beyond language. This is where the mood board comes in.

Create a multidimensional mood board

It's time to tap into your inner artist. To expand on the words in our little solar system, I like to create a "mood-board"—a collage that uses the senses and metaphors to abstractly portray the visceral feeling of the brand. This helps ensure that anyone who interacts with the brand doesn't just understand it on a cerebral level, but feels it in their gut. You should be able to look at it and almost instantly get the feel of the brand.

It's important that this be highly abstract. Don't choose images or objects directly related to your product or category. They should capture a feeling associated with the product, rather than the product itself. So if the brand is very comforting, maybe you show a snuggly blanket or a child held in her mother's arms. If the brand is whimsical, maybe you show a snarky smile or a TV/movie character that embodies that for you.

I call it "multidimensional" because this should be very free flowing and not limited to even visual images. This mood board can include anything that helps bring to life the brand and should borrow from different senses. Think about sights, sounds, music, people/characters/celebrities, movies, TV shows, objects, smells, places, events, and anything else that might cue the feeling you're after. There are no strict rules and the possibilities are endless.

You can even go beyond the page. I've seen brands create a physical room that you can walk into and experience the brand. Or maybe it's a bag of objects that sensorially and tactically convey your brand's feeling. A mood video can also work well. I'm using the term "mood board" or "collage" to refer to any of these forms, as the goal is to combine different things that together give you the sense for the brand. Feel free to be creative and have fun with this.

One tricky thing is that different people will have different interpretations of the brand and of the images and items

A mood board helps capture the feelings of a brand in a way that words cannot.

you use. So you'll have to try to find items for which there is a general consensus on their meaning and feeling. Editing is crucial here. Stay true to that feeling of the brand you captured in the meditation exercise and ensure that each item in your network and collage build toward that feeling. If something can be misinterpreted, take it out. You can also add short descriptors to items to make sure their reason for being there is clear. The goal is to have this stand on its own, without the need for much explanation.

The trigger

Lastly, I suggest finding a "trigger" word or phrase. You should do this last, because the process of building the rest of the Fantasy will help elucidate and congeal it in your mind. The trigger is your catchy phrase or line that can stick in employees' minds. It should be pithy, provocative, and aspirational for the brand—where it wants to go, rather than where it is today.

Too often, brands have something at the top of their brand positioning (the One Word Equity, Vision, Core, Essence, and so on) that then becomes the *only* thing that the brand is about. People that work with the brand only think of that one word or phrase and take their own definition of it, which can cause confusion among marketers and agencies. I'm calling this a "trigger" because it's not meant to be the whole idea or to stand alone. It's meant to be a reminder that brings to mind the rest of the Fantasy represented in the other pieces: the core words, fantasy network, and collage. It should trigger that full, rich feeling in the reader.

This trigger can also take many forms. It can be a single word, an object, a feeling, a verb or a noun, or whatever else. The only requirement is that it helps conjure up the rest of the Brand Fantasy. Although you're generally only talking about a few words here, they can be very difficult to write. Narrowing down on that key phrase or idea is tough, but can be super helpful when you are later working with marketing materials and need to check it against your Brand Fantasy. Recall your trigger, feel the brand, and ask yourself if what you are doing helps build that feeling.

Check your Fantasy against the Three Cs

As you create your Brand's Fantasy, make sure it aligns with these Three Cs: *consumer, commerce,* and *culture.* These pillars will ensure the Fantasy is relevant to your target market, is differentiated amongst its competition, and fits within larger cultural trends.

Consumer: It should fit with your target audience

Consumers are buying into a better version of themselves through your product or service, so your Fantasy should represent a personality, vibe, and attitude that your target audience aspires toward. It's a feeling they want to tap into and want to identify with. Your brand should be a part of their personal identity and how they want to see themselves.

Commerce: It should fill a gap in the marketplace

The Fantasy should be clearly differentiated from your competition. This is what is going to get people to choose your product over theirs. In fact, it's a good idea to also do this for your key competitors, so that you can clearly see where you are similar and different from them.

Culture: It should fit with today's and tomorrow's trends

This Fantasy should fit in the broader world, beyond your category and industry. It should make sense with macro-forces and trends that are shaping people's beliefs and desires today and in the future. It's also a good idea to find a group or subculture that has these beliefs and attitudes already, as it can be great to align with them as your influencer target.

You should also keep these tips in mind as you build the Fantasy for your brand:

- **Keep it dynamic.** Unlike other brand documents, this is not the kind of thing that you do once, laminate it, seal it with blood, and never change it. It should feel like a living, breathing thing. It should evolve as the feeling of the brand evolves. And because the world and people are always changing, your brand also needs to change to keep up.
- **Set a future vision.** It's where you want to take the brand, not a reflection of where it is today. It becomes your guiding light for everything the brand does.
- **Think about what you're pushing against.** It also helps to think about the opposite of your brand. What is its enemy or tension? What does it go up against? These can help you clarify what you stand for and what your feeling is.
- **Don't go it alone.** Although you'll probably need one main author to steward the Fantasy, you should get input from others who know the brand well, and from your consumers. You'll need to find the areas of overlap and consensus, so you know what the pillars of the brand are across people and not just in your mind.

- **Embrace the mess.** This won't be a clean-cut business document and it may never be perfect. Let go of those business rules and allow it to be a messy collection of associations and feelings that exist in your consumers' minds in a similarly messy and nebulous way.

————

There you have it. Though these exercises and documents may sound simple (or a bit whacky!), and a lot like some projective market research techniques you may know (not a coincidence), they can help add the all-important unconscious layer to the conscious parts of the brand you probably already know well. Use these as a guide to test marketing ideas or as inspiration to help create marketing materials, but in the end you will have a much richer and more complete

————————

𝒯his exercise should leave you with a rich brand world. You can think of it like its own culture, filled with its own people, personalities, sounds, smells, and tastes. For example, if you think of India, you can probably imagine a rich cultural world: colorful clothes, vibrant food and smells, signature musical sounds, and more. Now if you compare that image to New Orleans, you'd have a whole different set of sights, sounds, people, moods, food and drinks, smells and tastes.

————————

understanding of your brand if you acknowledge and bring out its hidden side.

Take Whole Foods. They sell food, but seem like so much more than a typical grocery store. They have clear values and beliefs you can talk about consciously, but they also have rich unconscious associations. The brand feels fresh, modern, hip, and healthy. You can easily imagine what a Whole Foods planet, party, or person would be like.

You want your brand to feel this way. You want to get immersed in it and feel like you can wallow around in it. Even the most simple and basic products and brands can have a deep and rich set of unconscious feelings and associations. This also works whether the brand is totally new and you're building the Fantasy from scratch, or if it's been around for over a hundred years. Either way, people will build associations and feelings with your brands. By going through this exercise, you'll be in charge of building those associations, rather than just letting them happen by chance.

Remember, this is not meant to replace how you currently think of and work with brands, but it is meant to add to it. It should add a layer of depth and richness that your consumers are feeling and are motivated by (whether they realize it or not), but that we typically ignore. Hopefully, this can create a more complete picture of the brand and be liberating and inspiring for those who work on it.

For tools, resources, and examples to help create your own Brand Fantasies, check out *www.daryl-weber.com*.

Takeaways

- The goal of the Brand Fantasy model is to bring the hidden, unconscious side of brands into the forefront, as these underlying feelings are critical to consumer preferences and purchasing decisions.

- The idea is to capture the nebulous and ethereal unconscious associations and feelings connected with your brand in a way that can be used and worked with by marketers and anyone involved in building the brand.

- Because we are translating the language of the mind, or "mentalese," into something more tangible, it will never be perfect, but it's as close as we can get.

- In order to capture your brand's feeling, you must first ensure you know it well yourself at an unconscious level. To break from the normal conscious associations, I suggest a meditation or self-hypnosis style session of introspection.

- My suggested pieces for the model include a trigger, core words, a fantasy network, and a multidimensional collage.

- The Fantasy should fit with the Three Cs: consumer, commerce, and culture.

- You should adapt this basic outline to whatever suits your brand and complements your existing brand documents and processes. These are not strict rules.

CHAPTER 8

The Brand Fantasy in Action

A Few Case Studies

Now that we've seen how the Brand Fantasy can be captured on paper, let's take it for a spin in the real world. In this chapter we'll see how a few successful brands harness the power of unconscious brand associations in the wild.

In choosing the brands here, the most important factor was, naturally, that they each have an exceptionally strong Brand Fantasy. That is, they must possess a rich set of unconscious associations that have set the brand apart, helped fuel exceptional growth, and built powerful loyalty amongst their consumers.

I chose brands that have not relied on typical mass communications or direct, conscious messaging. Instead, these companies bring to life a unique brand world with everything they do. They fully and authentically live their brands and focus on products, design, and experiences that consumers connect with it. In other words, instead of *telling* you about their brands, they make you *feel* them.

In an effort to avoid the typical clichéd examples, I've decided to go with three relatively younger brands you may not have considered as much from a branding perspective: Warby Parker, Hendrick's Gin, and Squarespace. They've all built rich brand worlds that have created connections with consumers, allowed the brands to differentiate, and propelled their growth. Let's take a look at how they did it.

Warby Parker: A story of great literature and the blue-footed booby

What do fixed gear bicycles, Jack Kerouac, and blue-footed booby birds have in common?

Not much, except that they were all integral pieces in creating the Warby Parker brand. Warby Parker is a brand of eyeglasses and sunglasses founded in 2010 in New York City by a group of business students from the University of Pennsylvania's Wharton school.

From the start, they set out to build a different kind of eyewear company. They saw that glasses were extremely expensive relative to the cost it took to produce them, and that the industry was dominated by basically one manufacturer with the (somewhat dirty-sounding) name, Luxottica. Though other companies had tried selling cheaper glasses, and had tried selling online, neither strategy had taken hold. The team from Wharton felt the industry was ripe for "disruption" (as the kids say) and needed a new kind of brand to do it. They set out to create that brand.

In various media interviews, cofounder Neil Blumenthal has talked about how they built the Warby Parker brand from scratch, and its story should be an inspiration to startups and established brands alike. Although many entrepreneurs tend to brush off brand building in an effort to focus on building their product, structuring a business, and dealing with the million other issues entrepreneurs face, Blumenthal knew that building a strong brand from the start was key. He also rejected the prevailing wisdom of "lean startups" and producing a "minimum viable product," or "MVP," to test and refine. Instead, he believed that for Warby Parker to succeed, it would have to be fully formed at launch.

Though the idea, in the most basic terms, was to launch a brand of eyeglasses that sold online, Blumenthal conceived of Warby Parker as a lifestyle brand first and foremost. He thought it should live in the world of fashion, not the techy e-commerce world. As such, he knew the brand needed to have a very clear personality and soul. It had to have a look and feel that people would connect with, aspire toward, and love. In essence, he focused on building a Brand Fantasy from the outset.

And it was no small feat. As Blumenthal tells it, he and his team spent a year and half defining the brand before launching. Naming alone took six months. Interestingly, it sounds like Blumenthal and his partners used a process quite similar to the one I laid out in the previous chapter, and it has served them quite well.

In an interview with *Inc.* magazine, Blumenthal and cofounder David Gilboa tell the story of piecing together this very strong brand. They actually created a mood board, with a carefully curated collection of what they called "inspiration pictures." They held heated debates on the selection of these images, as Blumenthal describes in the interview: "Are we preppy? No, we're not preppy! Are we retro, or are we vintage? Luxury or quality? We'd expect to spend an hour talking about the inspiration pictures we'd clipped out during the week, and we'd end up spending four or five hours. We'd debate one photo for an hour, whether it was exactly on brand."

Images they settled on included one of a fixed-gear bicycle for its simplicity, classic design, and "radical reductionism." They also liked its symmetry, and how bicycles in general connected with the ideas of environmentalism and doing good.

Another image was of the blue-footed booby, an exotic bird from the Galapagos Islands that Blumenthal states "fully encompasses the brand." In his words: "It's special, and not everybody knows about it. It's humorous, because it gives these quizzical looks. And the name itself is funny, like ours. But there's also a style and sophistication to it: It looks like a penguin, with that tuxedo breast. And then there's the flash of color. Our core company colors, the gray and blue, came from this photo."

Then there's the name: "Warby Parker." Say it out loud. It sounds literary, stylish, distinguished, yet still light hearted. It sounds like the brand. In the six months they

A fixed gear bicycle and the blue-footed booby were two concepts that helped inspire and shape the Warby Parker brand.

spent working on the name, they produced a list of more than 2,000 name options. In the end, Gilboa was inspired by a Jack Kerouac exhibit he saw at the New York Public Library. As he describes:

"He had written about all these characters in his private diaries, and they all had interesting names. There were two that all of us loved: Warby Pepper and Zagg Parker. We combined them and tested Warby Parker to make sure we weren't crazy. A lot of people thought it sounded familiar."[1]

In a field where competitors include names like the painfully literal FramesDirect.com and ThirtyNineDollarGlasses. com, they were clearly a fashion and lifestyle brand, not just a re-seller of frames.

Looking back on their process, it seems these founders were capturing a brand they already had in their heads and hearts, while sculpting and working it out via these external influences. It became a collaboration between their internal

visions and where they felt it needed to go. They then solidi-
fied this brand feel by creating internal brand guidelines and
writing style books that all employees keep by their desks.

Of course, those documents are confidential, but if I
were to describe the Warby Parker Brand Fantasy, some of
these words would come to mind: literary, witty, progressive,
cultured, modern. The brand has an air of sophistication to
it, without being pretentious. Its products are relatively inexpensive, yet the brand feels premium and stylish. Plus, the
company does good in the world, so you feel good making
the purchase. If I had to come up with a trigger to symbolize
and capture this overall feeling, I might call it "literary chic."
What would you call it?

A brand can't live only in internal facing documents. It has
to get out into the world so consumers can experience it and
start to build associations with it. Warby Parker was smart in
realizing that the brand was not just about the way they mar-
keted or even in the design of the products. The brand feel
they'd crafted had to inspire and guide *everything* they did as
a company. Only by doing that does a brand become true and
authentic, and consumers can feel the difference.

In addition to having well-designed, on-trend and stylish
frames (that is, a strong product) and a strong name, here are
some of the brand elements and activations that helped build
this brand feeling in consumers' minds:

- **"Buy a pair, give a pair."** Warby Parker
  launched with a social mission where every pair
  sold helps pay for glasses for someone in need

(taking a page from the Toms Shoes' book). This helps people feel good about the brand and makes it feel more progressive than traditional eyewear brands.

- **Virtual try-on.** They displayed their innovative spirit by creating a virtual try-on app that allowed customers to see how they might look in different pairs of glasses.

- **At-home try-on.** They went beyond expected customer service, offering an at-home try-on program: try on five pairs of glasses for free, including shipping. The hashtag #warbyhometryon made the program instantly shareable on social media.

- **Fashion week hush mob.** For very little money, the brand was able to make a huge impact in one of the world's most influential fashion events: New York Fashion Week. Rather than host an official event, they created a "hush mob" of models that took over a section of the New York Public Library during Fashion Week. The group quietly read (or pretended to read— we're talking about models here) bright blue booklets, and all donned Warby Parker glasses. The 40-plus editors and reporters that got secret invites to the mysterious event loved it, and all wrote about it. This ambush event was literary, stylish, clever, and very cheap. Brilliant.

- **Branded partnerships.** They partnered with cultural events that fit their brand, such as getting their glasses on that icon of glasses Clark Kent in a *Superman* movie, and holding a contest to win tickets to see the musician Beck perform in connection with his album that was released only as sheet music—very on-brand for them.

- **Physical experiences.** Before they had actual storefronts, they created a mobile school bus they called the "Warby Parker School Trip" to allow in-person try-ons.

- **Branded retail experience.** Their first storefront, located in the heart of urban style—New York City's SoHo neighborhood—was built to resemble a library. They even sell books in their stores today.

- **Selling a monocle.** Though I doubt they sell a ton of monocles, the fact that they offer it adds to the old-fashioned, dapper feel of the brand. This is a great use of a new product offering to serve as a brand building piece.

Warby Parker is a fantastic case study for any company looking to build a strong brand. They took a lesson from the fashion industry and created a complete brand world, very deliberately and thoughtfully, from the outset. It is now easy to imagine what a Warby Parker "planet" would be like, or if Warby Parker was a real person. The brand has a mood, an attitude, a feel, and a style. It has a personality that fits with cultural trends, differentiates it from the competition, and resonates with its target consumer. Although much of that can be conscious, most consumers probably give it little conscious thought. Warby Parker didn't have to tell us directly about how to feel about them, they just did it. Consumers now have this gut feeling toward the brand, picced together from all these different associations.

They upended the stodgy glasses category and succeeded where others had failed before them. I have to think this steadfast adherence to building a beautifully rich and deep brand from the start is at the core of their success.

Hendrick's Gin: A most curious tale, indeed

Not too long ago, gin was your grandfather's drink. Many young people today see it as the foul-smelling and harsh drink they stole sips of from their parents' liquor cabinets, only to instantly regret it and never try it again.

But for the past decade, gin has enjoyed something of a revival. Swept up by the craft cocktail renaissance, gin's role as the base for countless classic cocktails has breathed new life into this distinguished and debonair spirit. Gin producers, sensing that change was in the air, began developing a new type of gin for this new generation of drinkers— sometimes referred to as "new world" gin—that was lighter and more citrus-forward, and put the polarizing juniper flavor in the back seat. This style eases the transition for vodka lovers as they make the switch to gin (after all, gin is the original flavored vodka).

Although many of these new style gins have emerged since the early 2000s, one brand in particular has led the charge, introducing new drinkers to the gin category and gaining mass acceptance along the way. That gin is Hendrick's.

Gin may seem stodgy today, but the spirit has a rich history that recalls both the class (and degradation) of Victorian England, as well as the glamour and glitz of the roaring 20s and Jazz Age in America. Though many brands have tried to tap into this past to make the spirit relevant again, so far, Hendrick's stands above the rest. This brand has done many things well, but I would argue that a primary driver of its success has been the superior Brand Fantasy it has built.

It starts with the product itself. Rather than being another generic gin with an unknown mix of botanicals and flavors, Hendrick's took a bold stand and called out two unique flavor elements that it would become known for: cucumber and rose petal. To consumers that don't know much about the category, this wasn't just another gin, it was the "cucumber flavored" gin.

And cucumber has a British sensibility to it, calling up afternoon tea with delicate cucumber finger sandwiches—a lovely association for a British gin. They also began serving Hendrick's martinis garnished with a slice of fresh cucumber, a much lighter and more welcoming stand-in for briny olives. That simple and subtle twist gives the drink a cleaner, fresher, and more modern appearance and taste.

The Hendrick's packaging design also represented a departure from typical gin bottles. The short, squat, opaque black bottle with a diamond-shaped label and Victorian-era font gave the brand an old-world, apothecary look. It feels like a medicinal potion, with mysterious properties lurking within.

The name also fits well. "Hendrick's" sounds appropriately masculine, reputable, British, and personable. It makes you wonder (even if subconsciously), "Who was this Hendrick, and what makes his gin special?"

Together, these elements—the cucumber and rose flavors, the apothecary-style bottle, the name, and the premium price—already build a pretty strong Brand Fantasy

The Hendrick's bottle design defies category conventions.

in the mind. Hendrick's has provenance; it feels like it's from a place and is grounded in an aura of British heritage. It has a quirky eccentricity about it. It has an unexpected style and an intriguing personality. It is even a bit surreal. It recalls a Victorian era past, while feeling decidedly contemporary.

This Brand Fantasy fits well with its target consumers. The Victorian styling matches perfectly with hipster fashion of today: waxed handlebar mustaches, pinstripe vests, and pocket watches (perhaps even a monocle from Warby Parker) fit in as well today as they might have in 1800s Scotland.

Interestingly, although the bottle says "Est. 1886" on it, that was the year the parent company, William Grant and Sons, was founded, not Hendrick's. They focused on Scotch and only launched Hendrick's in the year 2000. But for this brand image to work, it's much better to think of the brand as being authentically from the 1800s—and I'm sure no one bothers to check.

Together, these elements create a rich brand world. One can easily imagine what the Hendrick's "planet" would be like (eccentric, slightly outlandish), who the people would be (old-style Scotsmen), what they'd be wearing (monocles, vests, handlebar mustaches), and even the sounds and smells (cucumber sandwich, anyone?). A trigger phrase for this Fantasy could be something like "Eccentric Victorian" or "Quirky Class."

They have continued to build upon this Brand Fantasy with clever consumer communications and experiences that support and embellish it. These tend to focus on the idea of "curiosity," a great word for this brand, especially when said in a British accent. It allows the brand to be strange, full of wonder and delight, and cue up the Fantasy world the brand embodies. Visit their website and you'll see what I mean.

A great example of this type of consumer experience is the pop-up events they put on in various cities around the United States called the "Emporium of the Unusual." To imagine it, start with one part gin cocktail tasting, one part Cirque du Soleil carnival, add a twist of taxidermy, and shake until you're thoroughly confused, but highly entertained. As the invitation stated in its cheeky tone of voice: "In cheery defiance of the mundane, Hendrick's will curate an assemblage of curiosities for the mind and palate. Might we inadvertently shift the world's balance of the normal to the odd? One can only hope. If anything is certain, it is that this will be a most enjoyable experience over cocktails."[2]

Of course, no one that has experienced these events believes this is truly what the brand is about. It's not very authentic, really. They are putting on a show and it's meant for entertainment. And I'm sure if you asked fans of the brand why they drink it, you'll hear things like "It's smooth," "I like the cucumber taste," and other aspects of the liquid itself. No one will admit to, or more likely even realize themselves, that maybe this highly differentiated brand is connecting with them unconsciously. Though the cucumber and rose petal botanicals are nice touches, I doubt most drinkers can really pick out these subtle flavors (there are still many other botanicals and flavors in it, including the ever-present juniper, which legally must be the prominent flavor for it to be called gin).

Notice that neither Warby Parker nor Hendrick's have very clear or overt conscious messages in their communications. They both have conscious aspects to their brands (for example, Warby Parker has its buy-a-pair-give-a-pair program, Hendrick's has its cucumber and rose petal flavors, and its "curious" messaging focus), but the real power of these brands lies in the less overt associations. Consumers are drawn to each brand in their entirety, to their rich world of associations, whether they consciously think about Warby's "Literary Chic" style or Hendrick's "Quirky Class" or not. This is why I say that to limit a brand to a one dimensional, singular idea or positioning is to do it a disservice and will leave behind much of the richness that is creating the strong brand aura in the first place.

Squarespace: The power of beauty

Until recently, building a website was an arduous task. You could learn web development yourself, or hire someone to do it for you. Both options cost money, take time, and who knows if you'd be happy with the result. Seeing an opportunity, a number of companies have sprouted up during the past few years that allow individuals and businesses to create their own websites, easily and simply, with no technical knowledge necessary. Some of these companies include

Wix, Shopify, Strikingly, GoDaddy, and Weebly, among many others.

As the space became highly competitive, a marketing arms race began to escalate, culminating in American marketing's zenith: Super Bowl ads. And out of this very expensive battle, one company is beginning to establish itself as a deeper and more meaningful brand in a sea of similar products: Squarespace.

All of these sites offer easy site builders for the technically challenged (like myself). They're all optimized for mobile, tablet, and desktop viewing. They all link with social media and help with SEO. They're generally pretty inexpensive; what used to cost tens of thousands of dollars can now be done for around $5–$30 a month, depending on your plan. Many even allow you to create an online store, with full e-commerce capabilities to sell your products.

Squarespace does all of these things. The nuts and bolts of its product are roughly the same as many of its competitors. But it feels very different. It doesn't feel techy like some, or too corporate and business-y like others. Instead, it feels impeccably clean, light, and airy. It's beautiful and elegant. Much like Apple, Squarespace has focused its brand on beautiful design, simplicity, and ease of use.

Design tends to be an afterthought for most companies. It's something they do at the end of the process, when an idea or concept already exists. But brands like Apple, Squarespace, Method, Target, and others, show how the right design doesn't just enhance or communicate your brand, it *becomes* your brand.

Without its unique design, Squarespace is just another website builder. As the founder and CEO Anthony Casalena put it in an article in *Fast Company* in 2014: "None of the products out there took style or design into account—which doesn't work when you're trying to build your personal identity online. Your website is where your ideas live. It reflects who you are. And all there was out there were these geeky, bargain-bin sort of services charging $2.99 a month for clunky experiences."[3]

The idea was to deliver better style, both in the final websites that its customers were able to create, and in how the Squarespace application itself looks and works.

You can see this emphasis on design and aesthetics in everything they do. Their website templates are beautifully designed, of course. The way you build your website and manage its back-end feels seamless and stupidly simple. They take customer service very seriously; you'll get a real person giving you as much help as they can in a clear, friendly, and informative way. Even their checkout system and automated e-mails are clean and simple. Together, all of this makes the tedious task of building a website actually feel like a refreshing cool breeze.

Squarespace also focused its aim on a specific target customer: creative types. Rather than trying to be for everyone (like most of the other website builders), they knew their focus on aesthetics would appeal to those that cared about good design. That's a deep shared value between the company and its users, which helps forge a strong connection. And then, once they built a strong following within the creative community, Squarespace was able to expand and bring in more mainstream users who want to be part of that community.

So Squarespace's Brand Fantasy revolves around elegant simplicity and beautiful design. It's a Zen-like experience. It's calming and focused. It reminds me of new-age spa music and maybe a cool sip of fresh cucumber water. I can imagine its mood board: clean open spaces, clear blue skies; maybe a Japanese tea ceremony, or bonsai plants; yoga poses; harmony and serenity. I'd also include some finely engineered products—like the sharp edge of a razor—to show precision, attention to detail, and functional expertise.

It's a beautiful brand image and one that feels very different from competitors like Wix or Shopify. Though Squarespace consciously highlights its focus on design (their current tagline is "Build it Beautiful"), these underlying feelings of airy simplicity and elegance sit beneath the surface, attracting customers and fueling its continued growth.

———

If we looked at these three brands from the traditional marketing point of view, the case studies would look very different. We'd focus on the conscious elements of the brands and miss much of the unconscious richness that has played an important role in each brand's success.

For Warby Parker, we'd talk about its at-home try-on offering, its low-cost products, its buy-a-pair-give-a-pair program, and we'd give a mention to its hipster style and designs. Although some of these elements are "emotional," I'd argue they still live in the world of the conscious. The traditional view wouldn't place much emphasis on the feeling of "literary chic," that modern, progressive, cultured sophistication and style are not just accessories, but *fundamental* to the brand.

*T*raditional marketing thinking would place less significance on the powerful unconscious associations connected with these brands, and in doing so would blind us to much of what makes each brand so strong.

Similarly, for Hendrick's we might mention its unique flavoring, standout bottle, and its experiential advertising campaigns. But then we'd miss all of the quirky, eccentric, British oddities that make the brand feel so different in the category.

As we saw in Part I, it's those underlying feelings for brands that guide our lazy, autopilot brain to choose one brand over the other. We go with our gut, and these brands have built very strong gut feelings.

*T*akeaways

- Traditionally, marketers have looked at the conscious elements of the brand (which include "emotional" elements), but have ignored the all-important unconscious associations and feelings brands build in consumers' minds.
- Warby Parker built a very strong brand carefully and deliberately. They planned their brand from the start and knew exactly what it would feel

like, even at deep unconscious levels. They prioritized this and it has served them well.

- Hendrick's pioneered the revitalization of the gin category by creating a brand look and personality that feels very different from other gins.
- Squarespace has achieved tremendous growth by creating a company built around a singular focus on beauty, simplicity, and ease of use. Although its competitors try to also have beautiful website templates, none have been able to fully own it in the same way. This has allowed Squarespace to get a strong hold on the influential creative class, which makes the brand aspirational to others.

PART III

Building Brands
That Seduce

Introduction to Part III
Building Brands That Seduce

In Part I, we looked at how our perceptions, attention, memory, emotions, and decision-making work in the brain, and how they can all be powerfully influenced by unconscious processes. In Part II, we applied this thinking to brands by building the Brand Fantasy model as an alternative to the traditional, more conscious-focused, brand models.

Now, for the last section of the book, we'll look at how marketers of all kinds can apply the power of the unconscious when building their brands.

Before diving into it, I want to address some of the ethical concerns that often arise when talking about applying neuroscience to marketing practices. That kind of talk can induce fears of Big Brother-like mind control, where companies begin tricking consumers and turning them into zombie buyers of their products.

I don't think those fears are entirely unfounded. As we have seen, we humans are not as conscious and rational as we like to think, and our lazy brains will usually take the easiest path, which tends to mean following our unconscious pulls. This means we are pretty susceptible to unconscious manipulation. Countless psychology studies show that we can be influenced by factors outside of our awareness.

That means, as it does in many aspects of business, that it's up to the companies and regulators to make sure ethical practices are followed. As the field of neuromarketing gets more established and more widely used, we'll need to better define where we draw those lines. I'm sure we'd agree that it's okay for retailers to play music that keeps us shopping longer, and for Subway sandwich shops to pump out their delicious freshly-baked bread aroma to lure in customers, but at what point do the practices that tap into our unconscious become unfair tricks? This will be an ongoing debate, but one where I believe laws and guidelines should be set up (where they're not already), so that we consumers can be in as much control as possible.

The positive side of this, however, is that by imbuing our brands with rich Brand Fantasies, we can add real value to the product or service for consumers. Much like how we get more enjoyment from a wine that you believe to be more expensive, a brand with a stronger Fantasy will be more satisfying, more appealing, and more enjoyable. Consumers get more out of it, and companies can charge more for it. It's why a piece of jewelry that comes in the light blue Tiffany's box can feel more special and exciting, or why the same shirt with a Nike swoosh on it can feel more motivating. Even if these are only perceived differences, when it comes to the mind, perception is reality. In that way, better brands actually give us better experiences.

The types of techniques I will be discussing in the following chapters follow this line of thinking—they're not at all about deceiving, but rather about building stronger brands that consumers will connect with more. It's up to marketers to act ethically, but I believe these tools make us better and smarter marketers, and more in control of the brands we are trying to build.

In Chapter 9, we'll take a broad view of marketing and look at all the nuances that can have profound impacts on how your brand is perceived. Chapter 10 will then look at how we can craft better communications and advertising that build the brand associations we'd like to have. Chapter 11 will discuss market research methodologies that can be used to better understand the hidden connections to your brand. Finally, we'll look at new product development from the perspective of the Brand Fantasy in Chapter 12. As each of these have a particular focus, feel free to skip the ones that don't apply to you and focus more on those that do. I won't be offended.

CHAPTER 9

Filling Your Brand Bucket

Aligning Every Piece of Your Brand to the Same Fantasy

Someone answers the phone on the first ring. A real, live human. He talks to me like a normal person, having a regular conversation. No scripts. No corporate speak. What's the best part? I feel like he really wants to help me. He actually cares.

This shouldn't be impressive, but it is. In today's world of automated telephone systems and lackluster customer service, this kind of warm, human connection feels sadly scarce. In this case, the friendly voice on the phone is helping me fix a mistake I made when trying to return a pair of sneakers I bought on the e-commerce website Zappos.com. It was my mistake, not theirs. But that's okay; he's going to help me figure it out. And he does. I end the conversation not just relieved, not just satisfied, but impressed and even a bit (could it be?) happy. When was the last time a call with a customer service rep made you smile?

Zappos does many things well. But one major contributor to its success has to be its emphasis on stellar customer service. Since founding the company, Tony Hsieh knew that to make ordering shoes online a reality, he'd have to have outstanding customer service. Today, that focus has become a central tenant of the Zappos brand. You can now order anything online from any number of e-commerce websites, so what's going to make you pick one over another? Assuming prices are kept roughly constant (which they typically are), that warm fuzzy feeling I got from my return experience will keep me returning to Zappos.

That's a moment of great brand building—it builds a strong, emotional association in a consumer's mind. But did it come from the marketing department? Not really. It came from a company-wide culture that started with the founder's relentless focus on delivering a great experience. It's not an "emotional benefit" from the marketing team or ad agency. It's not a positioning statement or marketing campaign. It's ingrained. It's core to who the company is, and it permeates everything they do.

The point is this: the responsibility for building a strong brand does not fall to the marketing department. "Branding" is not only for designers or creative agencies. Building a strong brand comes from *every* aspect of the organization, working together to create one unified whole. The business is the brand and the brand is the business.

Throughout the book we've talked about how every little thing that touches a consumer in connection with your brand is part of building your brand. Each piece, from your customer service, to your company's culture, your distribution, product experience, and everything else adds one more bit of information that your consumers add to their unconscious pile of ideas and feelings in relation to your brand. All of this helps build the network of associations and the feeling of your brand in their minds.

That means everything you do as a company is branding. Everything.

Think of it this way. Your brand starts out as an empty bucket, waiting to be filled with associations. At first, it's just an empty mental vessel. But with each and every interaction with your product and business, your consumer plops one more little association in the bucket. Though they don't realize it, they carry this bucket around with them all the time and whenever they encounter your brand, your competitors, or anything even related to your category, they add and change the contents of the bucket. As the owner of the brand, it's your job to make sure the bucket gets filled properly; that all the pieces point toward the same feeling, belief, and idea.

In this chapter, we'll go through a few of those pieces that together help fill that bucket and create a unified Brand Fantasy. These include the product itself, its name, design, price, and placement. These core aspects can set expectations and anchor all of the other associations you'll try to build with your brand.

Building a coherent whole

The Brand Fantasy, of course, starts with your product or service. You can't build a powerful aura or set of strong associations if they have nothing to hold them all together and hang on to. But it's not just the functional aspects of your product or service, it's the experience, and importantly, the *perception* of that experience, that matters most. How you talk about it, how you set expectations, how you define the experience and context, will all influence how people will see and experience your product, and how they build associations around it.

Today, most products and services are roughly the same. Can you spot a significant functional difference between Delta and American airlines, or Samsung and LG smartphones, or Dial and Ivory soaps, or Dropbox and Box.com? Pretty much every established category has a set of main competitors with very similar sets of features, benefits, options, and prices. Aside from occasional promotions or recent innovations that will most likely get copied very quickly, there is little to differentiate most brands from a functional perspective. After all, every washing machine will clean your clothes, every water brand will refresh and hydrate, every smartphone will have mostly the same apps, and every airline will get you where you're going with about the same rate of annoying delays.

However, in each of these categories, some brands have managed to carve out very different spaces, and feel very different, even if functionally they're about the same.

Virgin Airlines, and really Virgin as a whole, is a great brand despite not being known for having particularly great or award-winning marketing. Instead of *telling* you about its brand through marketing, it strives to *do* things differently in every way it can. The total product experience feels very different, even if it's still an airline flying the same Boeing planes and getting you to the same places as everyone else. They've imbued a sense of cool, modern trendiness and style into every aspect of the experience. When you step on board, they're playing curated music from DJs, have colored mood lighting, and the attendants have real personality (not canned, fresh-from-a-training-course personality). And of course, having a high profile founder like Richard Branson adds to the brand's intrigue, style, and pioneering spirit. Even their recent safety-video-turned-music-video has more than 10 million views on YouTube.

I can't recall a recent ad campaign for Virgin, or tell you what their "brand idea" is, or even what their slogan or tagline is. But I can tell you the brand overall feels ultra-hip, rebellious, and even sexy. They managed to do this in one of the most staid and corporate of categories plagued by tight profit margins, cut-throat price competitions, and safety concerns.

Or take Red Bull, the ubiquitous energy drink that launched the category and spawned an army of copycats. When it first launched, it was truly different. It had a strange name, was made with strange ingredients, and came in an oddly shaped slim can. And in the beverage category that preaches "taste is king," it tastes pretty damn bad (as blind tastes tests with consumers will tell you!).

But those all added to its intrigue and mystery. It felt like some kind of illicit, imported, slightly dangerous elixir. It stood out and felt like nothing else. Even its bad taste—which should be a negative—actually helped build the idea that this was something different and had a power to it. It tastes almost medicinal and feels like it must be doing something. (The same holds true for Jägermeister—its foreign name, bitter taste, strange bottle, and so on all imbue it with a sense of exotic power and mystery that helped make it the shot of choice for a generation of drinkers.)

Great brands like Virgin and Red Bull have built these powerful perceptions and associations through every part of their product experience. But importantly, each of these elements—product experience, name, company culture, design—builds on a single central theme. Each part adds to the same Brand Fantasy, so that it continues to crystallize around a certain set of feelings. All of the associations point in the same direction and build one coherent whole.

In psychology, this idea is called *cognitive consonance*. It's the opposite of the more commonly known cognitive dissonance, where conflicting ideas cause anxiety. Consonance is when the different elements fit together in harmony. This is how you want your brand elements to work—each one is a small piece of a large puzzle, and each piece plays a role toward building that one main mental image. As marketers, we have to know what the completed puzzle should look like (the Brand's Fantasy) and how all of the individual pieces contribute to building that image and feeling.

The art of naming

"Darth Vader." The name on its own sounds evil, sinister, and threatening. Even if you've never seen the *Star Wars* villain's metallic black face mask or heard his creepy breathing, the name alone just feels mean.

It shouldn't sound like much at all; neither "Darth" nor "Vader" are actual words in English. They don't have any direct meaning themselves. But they sound like and cue a host of evil associations. "Darth" sounds like a combination of "dark" and "death." "Vader" reminds us of the word "invader," and in a clever twist, even sounds like "father" in German. Together, without using an actual word, his name subliminally primes us for thoughts of darkness, death, and insidious invaders.

That might be an extreme example, but it shows the power in a name. A good name can help solidify and anchor your Brand's Fantasy with the right set of associations before you've said a word about it. "Zappos" sounds fun and friendly, is fun to say, and comes from the Spanish word for shoes, "zapatos." That's perfect for their focus on creating a warm and friendly customer experience in selling shoes.

The consumer packaged goods giant Procter & Gamble (P&G), though incredibly successful with many leading brands, is not generally known for creative, emotional, brand building efforts. More than most large consumer packaged goods companies, they've made a concerted effort to tout the functional benefits of their products in their marketing.

However, I'd argue they do some great emotional brand building in the way I've been describing—they imbue their brands with strong unconscious associations.

Take the dish washing detergent brand, Cascade. What does "cascade" make you think of? For me, I see clear, clean, fresh, rushing water from a pristine waterfall. If I could wash my dishes in a picturesque waterfall, I might actually do it; after all, what could be cleaner? Although I doubt many people ever think consciously about the meaning of the word "cascade" when choosing a dishwasher detergent, the priming research we discussed earlier shows that this kind of name should cue up and activate many of these kinds of associations (and what great associations to tie to your brand). Compared to competitors like Finish, Cascade starts with an almost unfair advantage.

P&G follows this formula with many of its category-leading brands. In cleaning products similar to Cascade, you have Tide for laundry detergent and Dawn for dish soap. Tide is similarly fresh, clean, and powerful. It reminds me of clean but strong crashing waves. Dawn, like the sun coming up over a dew-dripping field, feels fresh, renewed, and optimistic. How about Crest for toothpaste? Like the snowcapped peak of a mountain, it feels pure, clean, cold, bracingly refreshing, and fresh—perfect for the underlying feelings I want associated with toothpaste.

Though P&G tends to use real words as names, this still works for made-up words (or "coined names"), as well. P&G departed from using real words with their highly successful Swiffer product. "Swiffer" sounds quick (think "swift") and easy (the "er" suffix hints that it does it for you), which is exactly the idea of this new kind of mop.

In fact, research has shown that humans have a universal tendency to ascribe certain sounds with meaning. In a famous experiment from 1929, Wolfgang Kohler showed people a drawing of a loopy, round object, and a sharp, jagged edged object, and then asked them which one was a "baluba" and which a "takete." Although these are made-up words with no inherent meaning, 95–98 percent of respondents said the soft rounded drawing was a "baluba," and the sharp edged object was a "takete." This effect has been shown to span geographies, cultures, and ages, including 2-year-olds who can't read. This shows that though it may seem that words are arbitrarily placed with meanings, many words seem to naturally fit their meaning and have a sound that just makes sense.

Similarly, we should try to choose names that just sound right with our brand. Even if it doesn't have a literal meaning, the sound of the word itself should feel right for the product or service and the mood you are trying to imbue it with.

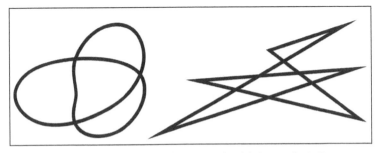

Which one looks like a baluba and which a takete?

Although we don't think about them consciously, these associations get activated when we hear these words and then become inextricably linked to our feeling for the brand.

A design is worth a thousand words

Graphic designers often understand a brand better than anyone else. They naturally grasp the importance of a brand's feeling and personality. They often use mood boards with abstract images to try to capture the essence of a brand, its mood, and aesthetic. They're used to delving deep into the significance of slight design changes—how a different color shade here, or a slightly different angle there, can change the whole feel of something. It's the marketers that tend to put the more conscious guidelines and guardrails on what designers instinctively feel works for a brand or not.

*M*any companies try to incorporate the benefits into the name or try to explain what it is. Although that can be helpful for really new or very different products that require some education, I'd argue that it's more important to cue the right set of feelings and associations. Capture your brand's feeling with the name, not just what it does.

Though designers may not think of this as unconscious branding and a network of mental associations, that is often exactly what they are creating with their designs.

Your brand's design is often the most tangible, most seen, and often the best encapsulation of what the brand is about. Whether it's a logo, package design, website, or anything else that visually represents your brand, it is through this design language that people get a first taste of your brand and build their impressions of its personality. As a very visual species, we humans can't help but judge books by their covers, people by their appearances, and wines by their labels.

By this point I hope you realize a brand is far more than just its logo or design (it seems that often still gets confused). Your design isn't your whole brand, but it's a representation of your brand. In much the same way I suggested you choose a trigger word when creating your Brand Fantasy model to trigger the rest of the Fantasy in your mind, your brand's design—its visual personality—serves as the trigger for consumers to cue up the rest of the Brand Fantasy in their minds.

Your design, no matter what it is, speaks volumes to the subconscious without saying a rational or conscious word, whether you want it to or not. This is true for every kind of design, even if you didn't think you actually "designed" anything. It's just like how even if you don't care about fashion or how you dress, whatever you do wear says something about you.

Although many brands have beautiful design, there are some for which design has been central to their brand and overall proposition (like Squarespace, discussed earlier). But a few brands have gone even further and have used the power of design to upend entire categories.

Method broke into the staid category of cleaning products and instantly stood out, carving out a new niche for itself. In a category dominated by large corporations with corporate-looking package design, Method realized that soaps tend to be displayed in the home, not hidden away like other cleaners. In addition to making environmentally friendly products, they designed their products to look far more stylish and modern than anything the category had seen before. This gave their brand an entirely different sensibility and feeling, which helped them quickly steal share and forced competitors to try to copy them.

Similarly, the brand Help Remedies, which makes super simple and friendly over-the-counter drugs, changed what we thought the pain relief aisle could look like. In an age

---

*E*ven what may seem like a terrible, cheap design can be endearing in that it can make a brand feel more approachable, more mom-and-pop, and less like a big corporation. Look at websites like Reddit or Craigslist. Most would agree that these (massively successful) sites have ugly, cluttered, difficult-to-use user interfaces and poor user experiences. They work just well enough. But for some, that may be part of the appeal—these homely sites feel like smaller, scrappier companies. Sometimes too much polish and overt "branding" can actually be a turn-off, and send people's BS meters buzzing. Our brains are quick to spot a hard sell and will put up defenses when they feel they might be being tricked.

---

of over-proliferation of products, big names like Tylenol and Advil created a myriad of options: Do I want gel caps? Should I get "fast acting" or "extra strength"? Or, do I just have a headache and want that gone? Help Remedies eschewed category norms and developed packaging that simply states your problem, such as "Help, I have a headache" for aspirin, "Help, I've cut myself" for bandages, and various other ailments. They gave the brand a fun, lighthearted personality in a typically very serious category. This came through not only in their design and naming, but in the stripped down products themselves, and in their tone of voice in communications. With a very small amount of marketing support compared to the big names, Help Remedies managed to build a

Method's groundbreaking design upended an established category.

strong and unique brand feeling through its whimsical design and tonality.

As these and many other examples show, your design can be worth more than a thousand words in explaining what your brand is about. It lets people instantly feel what your brand is, without any conscious thinking or trying. Design communicates no matter what, and it easily slides into consumers' set of subconscious associations connected with your brand. So make sure it's communicating not just the conscious elements of your brand, but that it imbues your brand with the feelings you want as well.

Context matters

Say you're on vacation at a beautiful beach resort and you happen to try a new drink while sitting outside. Your experience of that drink will be altered by your surroundings and current mood. In a way, that beverage will now be slightly associated with that sunny, warm day, the beautiful beach, and the good time you were having. Your brain will now link a hint of that vacation with that drink. Therefore, maybe the next time you're choosing a drink, you'll have a slightly more pleasant and favorable feeling toward that brand, and would be more likely to choose it than if you had first tried it sitting in an office eating lunch at your desk.

We don't experience anything in a bubble. As we saw in Part I, the brain is constantly soaking up much of what's around us, whether we consciously pay attention to it or not. When it comes to brands, this means that it's not just the product, the service itself, or their marketing communications that build the network of associations in consumers' minds. Everything surrounding the product experience gets encoded as well, and can add positive or negative associations to your brand, even if you as the marketer have nothing to do with them!

This has implications for distribution and sampling. If you try something at a cool, trendy hotel, some of that trendiness gets rubbed off onto the product you try. Let's say you see a brand of water first at a high-end spa or yoga studio. You might think about that brand differently than if you see it first at Wal-Mart. And because first impressions are particularly strong, where a product is first experienced will leave the greatest impression.

Starbucks is a great example of a brand that shifted the idea of coffee using contextual elements outside of the cup of

---

Although people certainly love Apple products, Apple has done a great job at everything that surrounds their products as well. Even the way their products are packaged is thoughtful, simple, and elegant, and creates a fun and exciting "unboxing" process. Their retail stores feel very modern and sleek, with friendly, non-commissioned "geniuses" that can help you. All of that imbues the brand with the right associations for Apple. (Though Microsoft tried to rip off that retail model with their recent stores, it reeks of copycatting and, therefore, doesn't help build a differentiating brand feel for Microsoft. It may even hurt them by having them be seen as copycats.)

---

coffee itself. They used exotic sounding names, higher prices, and created a comfortable, lounge atmosphere with pleasant music (if you're into that sort of thing) in their shops to move coffee from a cheap commodity to something much more special and premium. They redefined the category and built a strong brand in the process, without changing much to the coffee product itself, but instead adjusting everything around the product.

Changing the price changes the product

The price you pay for something can greatly affect how you perceive it. We tend to place higher value on items that are more expensive, think they taste better, and, amazingly, they can even *function* better through the placebo effect. A 2005 study by Baba Shiv at the University of Iowa showed that energy drinks that respondents thought were more expensive caused a greater physiological response than the same drink that was said to be discounted. Price in many ways tells our brains what to expect, and then that expectation meshes with the reality of the experience, even affecting the physical efficacy of the product.

We saw this with the Ketel One brand earlier. Although its package design cues authentic, old, and foreign, those things didn't fit with the current feel of the super-premium vodka category, which has a design aesthetic that was mostly cold, minimalist, and sleek. But when you combine that older, robust imagery with the high price of Ketel One, suddenly it put those design elements into a premium context. Instead of seeing the brand as outdated or dull (as they might have if it were cheaper), the higher price makes Ketel One seem real, authentic, high quality, and for people that know vodka. The price changes how you interpret the same elements.

It's not what you say, it's what you do

Recently, the drugstore chain CVS put their money where their mouth is. They want to be known as a health-focused company, and realized that selling cigarettes in their stores ran counter to that mission. So they did the unthinkable and pulled cigarettes off their shelves, incurring a $2 billion annual loss in the process.

They could have told you they were a health company all they wanted. They could have taken out Super Bowl ads and posted it on billboards across the country. But would you believe them? I'd bet you'd continue to think they were just another drug store selling the same products as any other, but trying to say they were different. But by taking a bold action like this, and getting tremendous free PR for it (in addition to the ads they ran), they are proving to you they actually care. They are showing you they have beliefs and a point of view that guides them. They are showing you they have a soul.

As a potential customer (assuming you're a non-smoker and agree with them pulling cigarettes), if you hear that, it becomes another positive association with the brand, and maybe you're more likely to choose CVS when given the choice. So far it seems to be working, with revenue jumping nearly 10 percent by the end of 2014, the year they implemented the change.

Here's another example. The delivery company UPS says they "love logistics." But do they, really? They can say that all they want, but for most consumers, it sounds like just another marketing story.

Then I heard this: UPS trucks don't make left turns.

That sounds crazy. How can a company that drives hundreds of thousands of vehicles all over the world not make left turns? But turns out that UPS is obsessed with efficiency—really, truly, scarily obsessed with efficiency down to their number-crunching core.

UPS engineers figured out that waiting to make left turns caused trucks to get delayed, used more gas, and increased the likelihood of accidents. They estimate that they now make right turns around 90 percent of the time, and that this change has shortened routes by more than 20 million miles, saved 10 million gallons of gas, and reduced CO_2 emissions by about 20,000 metric tons each year. Not bad.

As a consumer, knowing they are that obsessed with details and efficiency makes me never want to work there, but also tells me that they must be really good at what they do. I now have associations of precision, efficiency, and perfection linked to UPS in my mind, even if only unconsciously. And when UPS says they "love logistics" in their advertising, it no longer sounds like an empty marketing message. They mean it.

———

In this chapter I've tried to lay out how a few fundamental aspects of a brand can help anchor and solidify its Brand Fantasy. Though marketers know these are all important elements, it seems they tend to downplay the significance of the unconscious aspects of each of these. It is not only how consumers react to these parts of your brand consciously that matters (and therefore what they tell you in focus groups), but rather the feeling and aura they imbue the brand with that matters. We should think more fully about every aspect of a brand and company that can touch consumers, as each plays an important role in shaping the unconscious feeling of your brand.

Takeaways

- It's not just the typical marketing actions that define a brand; it's everything a company does. It all adds to the associations linked with your brand.
- Therefore, everything the company does needs to be built around and support the same brand idea. Each piece should work in harmony to shape and solidify the Brand Fantasy you want to build in your consumers' minds.
- Your name should impart the right set of associations to your brand. Rather than being purely educational or functional, the priority should be on finding a name that gives the brand the personality you're going for.
- Design is the face of your brand and speaks volumes about your brand's personality. Make sure it communicates what you intend, because

it will subconsciously communicate, no matter what it is.

- Where and how your product is experienced will be inextricably linked to the brand, and will shape the unconscious associations with it. Distribution, online placement, who your brand is seen with, and so on will all mold the perceptions of the brand.
- It's not just what you say, it's what you do. People will trust your actions more than your words, and actions give your brand authenticity and credibility.

CHAPTER 10

Advertising to the Unconscious

Building your Brand's Fantasy Through Communications

It starts off slow. The screen pans over to a tight shot of a gorilla's face. The massive ape leans back, closes his eyes, and takes in the moment as we hear Phil Collins sing "I can feel it, coming in the air tonight." The captivating buildup continues and the camera pans out to show the gorilla is sitting at a drum set, preparing to rock his gorilla brains out. He cracks his neck, takes a deep breath, and comes in perfectly in time with the drum fill and starts to rock the beat. Alone in a studio, he's having an amazing moment. Nuanced facial expressions bring the emotions home, and he's sporting a Phil Collins-esque ear-piece to boot.

If you haven't seen this now classic TV ad from 2007 for the UK's Cadbury's Dairy Milk chocolate brand, you should stop reading right now and watch it on YouTube. It will be a minute and a half well-spent.

In fact, that was the idea. They didn't want to talk about their chocolate or its ingredients (the product). Or talk about how delicious it is, or how it will melt in your mouth (the product/functional benefits). Or even how fun it will be to eat, or happy it will make you (the emotional benefits). They didn't talk about any of that or about anything at all, in fact.

As Cadbury's marketing director Lee Rolston put it at the time, Cadbury's Dairy Milk brand was feeling "like the comfy sweater you keep at the back of the wardrobe."[1] Although the brand still had some love in it, its Fantasy was weak, passive, and dusty. The agency they hired, Fallon London, was briefed to "get the love back."

Logically, this ad makes no sense. A drumming gorilla? Sounds like something a stoned 20-something dreamed up (maybe that's what happened). It has no direct relationship to chocolate, and arguably any confectionary brand (or any brand that brings you a simple pleasure) could have produced a similar thing.

But Cadbury is the one that did it. They took a simple and ridiculous idea, and executed it with meticulous craft to create a highly entertaining piece of film. To the conscious mind, the ad says very little. Most consumers won't really think about it, but if they had to, maybe they'd get that Cadbury is just trying to have a little fun, and that's what their products are about.

The more likely scenario is that people see it, enjoy a fleeting smile, and get on with their day. What they don't realize is that their unconscious mind processed this bit of stimuli, saw Cadbury's Dairy Milk at the end (even if they can't recall that it was for Cadbury!), and this encounter slightly altered their memory network for Cadbury. Maybe their unconscious idea of Cadbury evolved to become a bit more fun. It now feels a little sillier, a bit happier, a bit more surprising, unexpected, and creative. Maybe they hadn't thought much about this classic brand for a while, and it now feels a bit more modern and culturally relevant. And all that might make them more likely to choose it. In fact, this clever idea took the stagnating brand and boosted short-term sales by 9 percent, with continued longer-term growth throughout the campaign.

If you look at the traditional way of advertising, this kind of campaign should not work. There is no "product role." It isn't "ownable" or proprietary; you could replace Cadbury with many other brands and it would still work (maybe candies, sodas, ice cream, cookies, and so on). There is no consumer insight or "tension." There are no functional or emotional benefits, no "bite and smile" shot, or any other advertising clichés.

It shouldn't work. But it did.

———

In many ways, advertising is still very much a mystery.

As the retail legend and advertising pioneer John Wanamaker famously said nearly a century ago, "Half of my advertising is wasted. The trouble is, I don't know which half."[2] Despite the reams of data we have today measuring everything from advertising returns on investment and effectiveness, the self-congratulatory advertising creative awards, and the academic journals on advertising research, it seems there is still a lot of confusion, debate, and disagreement on the basics for how advertising works. And as consumers will tell you, no advertising seems to work on them, and yet clearly it does.

Though I will in no way claim to solve or end this debate, in this chapter I hope to provide a new way of looking at, judging, and thinking about how advertising works in the mind. We'll take a new perspective on how advertising (across all media) subtly and subconsciously influences us and our purchasing behavior. My hope is that by acknowledging and building a better understanding of the unconscious side of advertising, we can become smarter and more effective marketers.

All advertising is subliminal

Subliminal advertising is a myth, right? As we discussed earlier, the infamous Buy Popcorn/Buy Coke "experiment" from 1957 was a hoax. But, as we have seen throughout this book, the unconscious mind is always working. It constantly scans and processes our environment, and uses that information to guide our motivations and actions in subtle but powerful ways that, most of the time, are not available to consciousness.

So it stands to reason that the information we garner from being exposed to brands and advertising (and we're exposed to a lot throughout the day) would seep into our unconscious and guide our feelings toward brands.

And by "information" I don't just mean the message of the ad, or even just the product or brand. I mean everything about the ad, including its mood, the colors used, the actors or models and the emotions shown by them, the music and sounds, and even the environment and context in which the advertisement was experienced. As I mentioned earlier, all of this background, tonal, and contextual information is called "meta-communication." Although meta-communication appears incidental and unimportant—and is typically an afterthought or not a consideration at all for advertisers—it seems this kind of information can have *profound* effects on how we build mental associations with brands and thus influence our purchasing behavior, even when we're not aware of it.

To be clear, the typical idea of "subliminal advertising," where hidden messages (such as "Buy Coke") are encoded into advertisements or hidden in movies, is the subject of some debate, but generally considered nonsense.

However, there are many examples of *priming* where simple words or images can be presented too quickly to be consciously registered, but nonetheless influence future actions. Importantly, these are always *single* words. There have not been many studies that show that exposing *multiple* words in short phrases or sentences were capable of producing the effect. Though the unconscious mind can process tons of incoming perceptual data from our environment seamlessly, it seems it is limited in what it can handle from a semantic perspective, and putting words together to garner meaning is just too much to ask.

So although hidden messages like "Buy Popcorn" aren't likely to work, there clearly are elements of advertising that are processed unconsciously and that do affect us. And it's very possible that these elements are as important, if not more so, in influencing behavior as the conscious messages we work so hard to craft.

This is why all advertising has a subliminal element to it, whether we mean to put it there or not. Every part of an ad communicates something and subtly changes the network of associations for the brand, whether it was intended or not. So wouldn't it be better to acknowledge that it's happening and try to plan and guide those influences purposefully and strategically? I think so.

It's not what you say, it's how you say it

"Storytelling" is a hot topic in advertising today. Brands don't make ads anymore, they tell stories (or at least they try to). And this makes sense. Humans have a long and rich oral storytelling tradition. Before the advent of writing, stories were the way knowledge was acquired and passed on from generation to generation. It makes sense that we would be hardwired by evolution to appreciate, understand, and listen to stories, rather than lists of facts or piles of data. Tell me a story and you'll engage my heart and soul.

But when telling stories, we still assume that it is our conscious mind we need to reach. We think we need to grab the consumer's attention and tell them something they can consciously listen to, understand, remember, and repeat back to us. This, as we have seen, is flawed.

Stories are still a great way to convey a message, and elicit strong emotions and engagement, which are still important.

But what is just as important, if not more so, is *how* the story is told.

So why do we focus the majority of our efforts in advertising on the what, rather than the how? I can see a few reasons. For one, it's simpler, cleaner, and easier to talk about the conscious elements. That's what we can all plainly see and it's what you can talk to consumers, your boss, and your parents about. It also plays into the conscious myth we still hold dear—that we are more in control of our actions than we really are. But, despite all of that, it's still not what matters most.

Meta-communication matters more than you think

Like the devil, meta-communication is in the details. It's the way in which something is told. In advertising of any medium—print, billboards, digital, TV, radio—it's the elements of the production that give the ad its tone and

---

*I*n public speaking, it's often said that people will only remember 20 percent of what you say. Unless we're taking close notes, we'll forget most of the points. Talented salespeople also know that what they say isn't nearly as important as how they say it when trying to close a sale. If you stand tall, use a clear and confident speaking tone, and appear smartly dressed, what you say becomes secondary. The *how* often matters more than the *what*.

---

personality. This includes things like: color, lighting, photographic and director's treatments, casting, body language and facial expressions, music choice and sound design, and the inflection and voice of spoken words. It includes design elements like logos and typeface, the production quality, and the setting, location, and context of the ad. Everything—even a blank page—communicates something.

Without saying a word, they speak directly to the unconscious mind and exert their influence on the perceptions of your brand.

Every communication will have meta-communication. We humans are hard-wired to perceive it, even if we don't consciously notice it. Evolutionarily, this was important; we had to be able to read the feelings and intentions of others around us to gauge if they were a threat, friendly, or lying, for example. So we've learned to look beyond the words someone says to us and read their posture, body language, the subtle shifts in their voice and tone, and facial expressions. Together, these nonverbal communications give us a feel for the speaker. We don't think about it or give it any effort; it happens automatically and subconsciously.

Whenever you've had a "sneaky suspicion" about someone, or you feel like you "just don't trust them" and can't put your finger on why or, conversely, you feel attracted to them and inspired or impressed by them, you've felt the power of meta-communication at work. I'm sure you've heard someone say "I'm sorry" when they clearly did not mean it. Their words said one thing, but their tone said the opposite. Which are you more likely to believe, their words or their tone?

For example, as viewers of a billboard ad, we may not think about the seductive look on the model's face, the clean, sleek white background she is floating in, or the modern feeling a sans-serif font lends to the headline. We may read and forget the actual headline, but our subconscious picked up on these nuances and they subtly affected our memory network for that brand. Our gut feel for that brand is now slightly altered, even if we paid it no real attention, or if we can't recall the headline, or if we can't remember seeing the ad at all. Despite all this, the ad may still have "worked" in some way. It still helped shape perceptions of the brand and build brand equity, which can help sell the product.

The message came and went, but the feeling remains.

The problem is that most of the time and energy spent on developing the ad was likely spent on that conscious message that was heard and forgotten, rather than on the underlying feeling created by the ad that endures and contributes most to the purchasing decision.

So I would argue that production development and quality are actually more important than most marketers realize. The detailed but crucial decisions of how a story is told and how it comes to life will be critical to the overall feel imparted to the viewer.

But rather than being part of the upfront strategy, these critical decisions are often left up to what feels right when you see it. I believe the role of meta-communication and the overall feel you want to imbue your brand with should be given far more emphasis and be clearly discussed as part of the goals of the advertising. It is in fact part of—and integral to—the strategy of the ad. "Strategy" should include the feel and tone as much as it does the insight, message, and brand role.

Remember that meta-communication is always there, always. Everything that is said is said in a context. Even plain black type on an empty white page says something about the brand. So let's decide what the meta-communication should say, as much as we decide what the overt communication should say.

Again, this is different from how most marketers today think of "emotions" in advertising. I'm not talking about bringing up an emotional topic (like, say, a parent's love for their children), or about ads that make us laugh or cry, or about ads that directly talk about the emotion they want you to connect with their brand. No. I'm talking about the unconscious gut feel that gets created by the *way* your brand communicates, and how that gut feel is then used to decide whether or not your brand gets purchased.

A brand's personality shouldn't be left to whim or "knowing it when you see it." How a brand feels to consumers is critical to its success, so it should be taken just as seriously as the other parts of a brand's strategy.

That can be far more powerful and "memorable" (if only implicitly) than any rational message. As we saw in Part I, these kinds of associations picked up from meta-communication work with our implicit memory, making them more durable, long-lasting, and exert more influence than rational messages that quickly fade away.

Getting attention may not be all that it's cracked up to be

I want to challenge another assumption in the advertising world, that for advertising to work, it must first get someone's attention. As discussed in Chapter 2, our attention is more layered and complex than the simple conscious "spotlight" we experience. We now know that our unconscious mind scans the environment and picks up bits of information, causing implicit learning to take place. So advertising can still have some effect even when someone pays very little or even no attention to it, which is what happens most of the time.

We often think that the role of the "creative idea" in an ad is to "break through the clutter," attract attention, and serve as a vehicle for the message. That can still work, but as we have seen it is unlikely to happen and can even backfire. Remember the discussion of Robert Heath's counter-argument, where consumers put up mental defenses the more attention they paid to an ad? Rather than letting an ad wash passively over them without putting up a fight, direct attention can actually cause us to question an ad more and pick it apart (just like consumers love to do in focus groups when forced to pay unnaturally close attention to ads).

However, the creative idea of an ad can serve another purpose that actually helps the brand idea seep through to consumers' minds. When ads are entertaining and we briefly get sucked into something, it can help lower those defenses and allow the message to seep through more easily.

For example, in the recent Super Bowl commercial for Volkswagen, a young boy dressed as a cute Darth Vader tries to use "the force" to do various things telepathically around the house. When he's outside trying his powers on his parents' car, his dad cleverly presses the remote start feature on his car keys from inside the house, turning on the car's engine and the boy's imagination.

From the points of view we have been discussing here, this ad does a few things very well. The creative idea—a boy dressed as a *Star Wars* villain trying to use the force— is entertaining and allows us to relax and let our marketing guard down. Though the Super Bowl is a rare occurrence in which many viewers watch the commercials with rapt attention, the ad brings us into the story and allows the intended rational message—the remote start feature—to be naturally integrated.

But also, and possibly more importantly, the feel of the ad adds to our sense for what the VW brand is all about. The ad and, therefore, the brand, feel family-friendly and approachable. It feels witty, clever, and has a sense of humor. Through the casting and wardrobe, it feels stylish, sophisticated, and for today's upscale modern family. The meta-communication tells us all of this, regardless of what our conscious mind was paying attention to (the story of the kid and his sought-after powers).

So we take away things from ads even when we don't pay close attention. We may not notice the Powerade posters in the background of a soccer match, but our minds will most likely see it and subconsciously make a slight connection between the FIFA World Cup and the Powerade brand. That connection can make the brand feel a bit more authentic to sports, more relevant to athletes, more contemporary, and more legitimate for being part of such a world-class sporting event. All of those associations can seep in with no overt message and no direct attention paid. Advertisers clearly know the value in these kinds of sponsorships and the air they can lend to brands, which is why they pay so much for them. But although we know this when it comes to sponsorships—simply adding a name or logo to something—we seem to lose sight of it when it comes to more direct forms of advertising.

When we're more relaxed and are half-ignoring ads (as would typically be the case when flipping through a magazine, scrolling online, passing a billboard, listening to the radio, or watching TV), we can let the ad wash over us, not think much about it, and move on. In most cases, people will pay the least amount of attention necessary. Remember, our brains are lazy and want to conserve precious energy whenever possible.

So if we don't think about an ad enough to counter-argue it, maybe the message actually seeps in *more* than if we paid closer attention. Ironic, no?

This changes the long-held belief that the role of the "creative idea" in advertising is to gain attention. Instead, the "creative" parts of an ad can serve to help lower our defenses and cause us to pay less attention to the message, not more. The story can entertain the viewer, making them more relaxed and less focused on picking apart an overt claim or message. This means that even if explicit brand or message recall are low in consumer testing, the relevant associations may still be getting through, even if only subconsciously.

This is contrary to much of what most marketers believe, but there is some strong evidence to support it. Though still a theory and more research is needed to fully flesh it out, I believe it is worth taking into consideration as a secondary way in which advertising can be effective.

The great product vs. emotions debate

Some call it "intrinsic" and "extrinsic." Beverage and alcohol brands talk about what's inside the bottle (the liquid) and what's outside (the brand). Some say functional benefits and emotional benefits, or maybe product role and brand values. Whatever you call it, if you've been involved in developing advertising, you've probably taken part in debates on whether to focus on product attributes or to make a more emotional connection, or more likely what kind of combination of the two is best. This ongoing debate never seems to end and everyone seems to have an opinion on it.

In general, it seems in recent years the advertising pendulum has swung toward emphasizing the emotional side, where the product gets only an obligatory flash at the end. Though they may now be falling out of favor, grandiose "manifesto" and "anthem" style films that boldly declare a brand's values and beliefs have been all the rage. This style talks directly about what your brand stands for, in an attempt to show your consumers that the brand's values align with theirs, so they should connect with and relate to you brand and in theory be more likely to choose it. Typically, the connection to the product in these ads is circuitous at best. They can sometimes be powerful, inspirational mantras that align their values to yours, or can sometimes leave you wondering what product it was for and why a shampoo is telling you how to live your life.

There has also been a recent trend dubbed "sadvertising" that aims to rip at the heart strings to the point of eliciting real, genuine tears from viewers. Somehow in advertising, regardless of the product, making your audience cry became seen as a huge success. It meant you were touching consumers emotionally and engaging them with a powerful message. Although that can be true, simply making an emotionally wrenching or provocative statement may or may not be lending the right associations to your brand. Yes, they grab direct attention and yes, they touch viewers emotionally at a conscious level, but the key question is *how is that helping build your brand equity unconsciously?* This is rarely, if ever, considered.

Though it would be impossible to solve this debate and give a clear-cut solution that would work for every brand, I think we can look at this issue based on the brain science we've discussed here and get at least a few clues as to what might work best.

As we have already shown, in order to build brand equity, marketers need to build the underlying feeling of a brand— the network of unconscious associations. So although sharing your brand's values, beliefs, and point of view can help do that, and those things are certainly important parts of what your brand is about and the feeling it will create in your audience, it is not the whole story. They are the conscious side, and the unconscious associations get built almost by accident.

On the other side, the product and its functional benefits also do play a role. Though there are some categories in which consumers will study product details (electronics, cars, homes), generally it seems consumers need a very simple, easy to understand, rational justification for their purchase. They want some easy way to validate the choice their gut is telling them to make.

With alcohol, maybe it's how many years a whisky has been aged. It's why Certs has "Retsyn," whatever that is. And why Coors Light made being watery into a positive by calling it "the world's most refreshing beer." A simple rational justification can go a long way and is all most people need.

So if you don't need to belabor product attributes, and you don't need to hit home the emotional (but still conscious) values and benefits, what should we communicate then? In my opinion, the role of long-term brand building communications (not promotional, direct response type communications) is to build the right unconscious attitude, feeling, and personality for your brand. That is the priority—to help build your Brand Fantasy.

As I said in the Introduction, fashion and luxury brands do this well. They don't bother talking about product attributes. Does a Rolex tell better time than a Casio? Is a Chanel bag really *that* much better made than brands at a tenth of the price? No, clearly these types of brands are all about the style, mood, look, and air of status surrounding the product. That is where the value is and that is what they are selling, far more than just a watch.

So their ads don't try to sell you on product features. Nor do they hit you with emotional benefits stating how great you'll feel wearing or carrying them, their point of view, or beliefs on the world. Instead, they create a fantastical world. They show gorgeous (if somewhat alien-esque) models prancing around in ridiculous situations. "Sure," they say, "let's throw a chicken in that print ad." Maybe it gives their brand a bit of country warmth and subversive edge at the same time.

Fashion and other "lifestyle" brands (the good ones, anyway) are masters at creating unconscious brand feelings. It's surprising that in other categories we get so focused on conscious product and emotional benefits that we ignore this side of it.

I hate to bring up the Apple brand again, but this is something they excel at. Throughout much of their recent advertising history, all they do is simply, beautifully, and elegantly tell you about their product. When the iPod launched, they said on bold but simple billboards, "1,000 songs in your pocket." They followed that up with wild street postings showing black silhouettes dancing against colorful backgrounds, with the iconic white earbuds dangling around the neck. These imbued the product with a lively, fun, dancing feel, without having to directly or consciously say anything at all.

Sometimes, just talking about your product in a "cool" way can work best. Again, by "cool" I mean whatever the attitude and feel that works for your brand and category.

The Apple brand stands for a lot—most notably the idea of "creativity." But they don't talk about this directly. They don't seem to ever even use that word in communications.

These ads imbue the product with emotions without saying a word.

However, everything they do imbues the brand with a sense of creativity. They tell us about their products in a way that makes them feel creative, inspiring, and for creative people.

The Mexican beer brand Dos Equis has had great success with its long-running "The Most Interesting Man in the World" campaign in the U.S. Being an import, I can see how this brand lends a bit (a tiny, tiny bit) of an exotic and worldly air to the person drinking it, at least compared to the all-American Budweiser guy. These ads tell the many tall tales about this hilarious character. We learn things about him like, "Sharks have a week devoted to him" and, "He has inside jokes with people he's never met."

Consciously, they don't tell you much of a message. But they do, through clever humor and great exaggeration, make the brand feel "interesting." You get a sense that the drinker of a Dos Equis will seem a bit more experienced and traveled than domestic brew drinkers, without saying it overtly.

I think consumers have gotten savvy enough about how marketing works that they can see through over-promising, overly lofty, or fluffy messaging. They know your app, service, or product isn't really going to change the world. So there is a sense of honesty and integrity that comes with being true to your product, but doing it in a way that imparts the right feelings to your brand. This new style—just talking about your product in an interesting and unique way—is where I believe (and hope) advertising is headed.

It's not about telling your Brand Fantasy directly. You have to tease it, seduce it, and bring it out in subtle, but consistent ways, across all media and brand touch points.

Takeaways

- All advertising will have "subliminal" elements to it, in that any communication will also have meta-communication that gets processed and stored subconsciously, and can influence our feelings toward a brand.

- Meta-communication is very important for building brands, but is usually not given much thought. The feelings imparted to a brand through its meta-communication will be more durable, longer lasting, and even more influential than the conscious messages that are often quickly forgotten.

- Although marketers spend a lot of time, money, and energy vying for consumers' attention, direct attention isn't necessary for meta-communication to come through and can often backfire due to the "counter-argument" effect.
- Marketers often debate how to blend product points and functional messaging with more emotional communications, but both of these are still going after the conscious mind. Sometimes, telling a story about your product gives consumers the rational justification they need, but telling it in the right style and attitude gives the brand the right emotional feel.
- Often in brand-building advertising, it's less about what you say (the conscious message) and more about how you say it (the unconscious feel).

CHAPTER 11

Researching the Unconscious

Market Research that Actually Works

You've probably been there. Bored, tired, and sitting in a dark room with only a bowl of M&Ms to keep you from stabbing your eyes out. It's the third group of the day and all you can think about is where you're going for drinks afterward to try to forget the misery of sitting through six hours of focus groups.

I can understand why the standard, fluorescently lit, painfully sterile, focus group came to be. We want to know what our target consumers will say about our new product idea, our new pack design, our new advertising campaign ideas, or whatever else. We want to hear what they'll say about it, so we can see if we're on the right track and how to make it better. It's logical enough.

So we stick a bunch of consumers in a room, video record them, and tell them to not pay much attention to the ominous one-way mirror with mystery people behind it watching their every move. Then we pay them to talk to us. Yeah, that's natural.

Aside from being an alien environment for consumers, and dreadfully boring for marketers, there's a much bigger problem with most standard market research—it doesn't work.

Despite reams of market research data saying they will be successes, the vast majority of new products fail (we all know the story of New Coke, right?), countless advertisements fail to reach their goals, and many brands miss the mark on their strategies.

The fundamental problem is that traditional market research assumes that consumers are capable of telling you why they buy something. It assumes we can ask the conscious mind why it does what it does, despite the mountains of evidence that much of our purchasing decisions are driven, at least in part, by unconscious processes. It's not that they lie; it's that we humans are just not able to look into ourselves and understand what's going on below the surface. Instead, we look for rational justifications, social cues, and other crutches to guess at what we would do. But they are just that—guesses.

We have to be more realistic about what consumers can and can't help us with. Getting some conscious reactions to marketing materials can be helpful in catching things that might cause a backlash on social media that the marketers missed, but it is very hard to ascertain purchase intent or desire from what people say.

Instead, marketers should attempt to understand the unconscious side of their ideas. In this chapter we'll discuss research techniques that can help uncover unconscious influences and aspects of your brand, and better help guide your marketing decisions.

The rise of neuromarketing

Perhaps you've heard the term "neuromarketing" thrown about. This burgeoning field has many definitions, but generally refers to the use of neuroscience understanding and technologies to improve marketing effectiveness. One of the major goals of these methodologies is to bypass the conscious mind of the consumer and get reactions directly from the brain itself. In a way, they are windows into the unconscious and inner workings of the brain.

These techniques are complex, but for our purposes I'll just provide a high-level overview of some of the more common methodologies. If you're interested, check out *www. daryl-weber.com* for more on neuromarketing techniques, books, and online materials that go into more depth.

- **fMRI:** Functional Magnetic Resonance Imaging (fMRI) uses powerful magnets to track blood flow in the brain as subjects are exposed to visual, auditory, or even taste cues. This works because when an area of the brain is in use, blood flow to that area increases. Although this can provide detailed views of the brain at work, it is very expensive, cumbersome, and uncomfortable for respondents.

- **EEG:** An electroencephalogram (EEG) uses small metal discs called electrodes that are placed on the scalp that monitor the electrical activity caused by the communication between neurons. This activity shows up as wavy lines, and can indicate general findings like when and if the respondent was engaged by a piece of stimulus, and if they have positive or negative emotional reactions to it.

- **Facial Coding:** Facial coding is the reading of very fast, fleeting facial expressions that serve as windows to the immediate, true emotional reactions of subjects to a stimulus. The idea is that immediate facial reactions are automatic and unconscious, so they show our true feelings, even if we try to hide or change them consciously afterward.

- **Eye Tracking:** Just like it sounds, eye tracking tracks the movement of the eyes, which can tell where a person is focusing and what they look at, which can help gauge intent and interest. It can also measure emotional saliency by measuring pupil dilation and blink rate.

- **Biometrics:** Biometrics is the measurement of the body's physical reaction to stimuli (facial coding and eye tracking can be considered biometric as well). Common techniques are similar to the lie-detector test or polygraph, where researchers measure heart rate, blood pressure, respiratory rate, and the galvanic skin response (a pre-cursor to sweating) to gauge general emotional engagement.

- **Implicit Association Test:** IATs measure reaction times of related concepts to gauge the level of association between the words or categories. More on this in the following.

The positives of these methods are that they can provide glimpses directly into the workings of the brain itself, without the need for consciousness or even language to get in the way and muddy things up.

There are some downsides as well. These techniques tend to be very expensive, so that currently only the largest corporations can afford them, and even then only with limited respondents. They also take place in highly unnatural environments, which can skew respondents' emotional reactions.

The biggest concern, however, is in the interpretation and application of the results.

Issues facing neuromarketing

The use of these neuromarketing methodologies has been controversial. One key issue has been that many neuroscientists bemoan the overpromising and exaggeration of the findings and feel neuromarketing isn't worthy of academic research.

For example, Martin Lindstrom, a brand consultant and author of the book *Buy-ology*, wrote a piece for *The New York Times* titled "You Love Your iPhone. Literally."[1] In it, he describes how an experiment showed activation in the insular cortex of the brain, an area, he claimed, is associated with feelings of love. He therefore made the conclusion that the respondents were literally in love with their iPhones. The problem was, as many neuro-scientists pointed out, the insular cortex lights up in about a third of all fMRI studies and is involved in many feelings, including disgust. This shows that we cannot draw backward, illogical conclusions like this from brain imaging studies, we shouldn't trust a single experiment, and ideas like this must be peer-reviewed to help catch flaws. We must be careful not to over-promise and exaggerate findings.

In this book, I have tried to take a different approach to neuroscience understanding. Rather than being a test at the end, I believe being better informed on how the brain works—and how marketing communications get perceived, stored, and used for decisions—can help inspire better creative ideas at the front-end of the process.

Whereas the scientists debate the validity of some of these findings, on the other end of the spectrum, the cre-atives in marketing have a very different issue with neuro-marketing. Because these techniques tend to be used to test communication ideas or designs at the end of the creative process, creatives tend to see them as idea and creativity killers, rather than helpers. They don't want the scientists telling them how to craft their ads, designs, and communications based on brain science. That isn't how art works, after all.

Lastly, neuromarketing raises many ethical concerns: Are marketers going too far? Are we "tricking" people, brainwashing them, or turning them into buying zombies out of their own control? As I have emphasized throughout this book, and as many great scientists such as Kahneman and Ariely have shown, clearly we are not as rational, nor as consciously in control, as we like to think. That, to me, shows that we are indeed capable of being exploited by marketing ploys. So I believe there is cause for concern; regulation is needed to ensure marketing does not trick people.

However, the conscious mind can still override the unconscious desires (even if it's difficult, like saying no to dessert). Also, like anything else, these techniques can be used for good or evil, and I believe most marketers do not want to intentionally trick consumers. So although I don't believe we are anywhere close to creating zombie consumers and brainwashing people, I do think the industry needs to be watched, and take great care to remain ethical as neuroscience understanding and neuromarketing practices progress.

Mining your brand's implicit associations

I want to call out one technique in particular that I think holds great potential for marketers trying to understand the unconscious associations with their brand—the Implicit Association Test, or IAT.

The IAT is based on the idea that concepts are represented in our memory as networks of interrelated ideas, not as single, stand-alone ideas, just like we discussed in Part I. If you recall, we looked at how when one idea in this interconnected network is activated, other related ideas will be activated as well. The IAT measures the strength of the association by testing reaction times for associated words. In the test, subjects are asked to hit buttons on a keyboard saying whether a word fits into a category or not, and the speed at which the answer is made can be telling. For example, if the idea of "Doctor" is primed, you are more likely to respond faster to the word "Nurse" than for the word "Singer." Though the differences in reaction times are in milliseconds, they have been shown to be quite significant and reliable in showing associations between concepts and categories.

The IAT measures implicit (unconscious) attitudes, beliefs, and associations with a given idea. Malcolm Gladwell famously wrote about taking a racial bias form of this test in his book *Blink*, where he discovered, somewhat uncomfortably, that he harbors a "moderate automatic preference for whites." (This shouldn't be that surprising, because 70 percent of people across races who take the test show this preference for white people.)

This test can be done over the Internet, cheaply and easily, and can give you insight into what ideas and feelings are associated with your brand. Although there is some controversy on how valid the findings are, the technique has been widely used in social and cognitive psychology, and some neuromarketing firms have been employing it with success. The IAT fits well with the idea of the Brand Fantasy: if every brand holds a set of unconscious associations in the mind, marketers would do well to have a better understanding of what those associations are and how closely they are linked to their brands.

To see an IAT in action, check out *www.daryl-weber.com* where I have links to a few different kinds of IATs that you can take yourself (they only take a few minutes). This can help you get a feel for the technique and even learn something about yourself in the process.

Using projective techniques to probe the unconscious

Despite the rapid growth of neuromarketing techniques in recent years, there is still a role for more traditional market research. When done well, qualitative research methodologies—especially those that use smaller groups and get outside of a focus group facility—such as ethnographies, in-depth interviews, friendship groups, observationals, shop-alongs, and others can paint a rich picture of the consumer, how they interact with your product or service, how it fits into their lives, and much more. They can also show you the conscious side of your brands, which is still important.

But in order to get at the underlying, unconscious aspects of your brand, design, or marketing materials, you often need to go a little deeper than just asking them. You need to go beyond ordinary language and conversation. The following are a few techniques I've found to be helpful in uncovering deeper, underlying insights and brand associations. These are generally referred to as "projective" techniques, in that they use indirect methods to try to get at the unconscious feelings connected with the brand. Notice that many of these are similar to the methods I suggested to build your own Brand Fantasy, which makes sense because they can help both you as the brand owner as well as consumers unearth deeper feelings about the brand.

- **Image Sorting/Collage Building:** Collages may be seen as cheesy, but I think they are a simple, cheap, and fun way for consumers to get past the logical and rational language, and feel free to tap into and express the mood of a brand—and that is golden. Giving consumers inspiration and stimulus with stacks of images or magazines (unrelated to the product category) can spur their thinking and force them into making more abstract connections that you would otherwise miss through standard questioning. This is how, for example, we were able to unearth the strong, bold, masculine associations with the Ketel One brand. It came out clearly in the collages, but was not mentioned at all in the discussion.

- **Personification:** Pushing consumers to think of brands as people can also help them get into the personality of a brand and away from the rational. We are used to thinking about people in terms of attitudes and behaviors, and in my experience consumers can have fun with this and really get into it. You can have them describe one brand as a person (for example, what they would be like, what they would wear, drive, do for work), what their relationships would be like, what their family would be like (and what other brands would be in it), and more. You can also suggest that if a group of brands are at a party together, how might they interact?

- **Planets:** I also like to push consumers to build out rich, detailed brand worlds. If the brand had a planet, who would be on it, what would the climate be like, what would the people be like, what would they wear, what would the culture and society be like, and so on.

- **Word Associations:** You can also do a simple word association game where consumers say whatever comes into their minds related to your brand. The moderator may need to push them to be abstract, but often random and unexpected things can pop up, especially once you get past the first few obvious answers.

- **Stories:** You can also have consumers make
up mini stories, fill in sentences, fill in thought
bubbles or cartoons, or write letters to the
brand. Techniques like these push respondents
to be a bit more creative and make lateral connections they otherwise might not.

There are many other projective techniques and you
can go much further in depth on moderating techniques to
extrapolate subconscious associations with brands, but I just
wanted to give a high-level taste for them here. In my experience, these types of techniques often lead to the richest and
most inspiring insights.

However, I should caution that proper probing and interpretation is critical. It's not just that someone puts an image
of an SUV driving through mud on their collage—you must
understand what they meant by it. Was it that the brand in
question feels rugged and tough, that it's liberating and free,
or that it's messy and dirty? So you have to probe on the *whys*
behind what they choose and ask them to explain.

But just as important as asking is the *interpretation* of what
they are saying, and this can be very difficult. This is where
market research becomes a bit of an art, where you have to be
able to read *behind* the words and images to see what is really
causing the person to say what they say, what they really mean,
and what it means for the brand. This can be very subjective, so
it's important to test your hypotheses in different ways and with
different people. When you see similar results across people
and techniques, you're probably uncovering a nugget of truth.

How to hear what consumers are really saying

We must be very careful when listening to consumers. We must look past just the words they say, which can be easily swayed by social pressures, group dynamics, the way a question was worded, or other factors. Instead, we need to read between, behind, and around the quotes, and pay attention to *how* they say what they say in order to get at the subtle and implicit aspects of the brand. Here are a few ways to do this:

- **Pay attention to body language.** Notice what gets them to sit up and engage, what makes them fold their arms and back away, and what brings the excitement level up in the room. These kinds of nonverbal cues can communicate what they're really feeling, even if their words say otherwise.
- **Listen to the tone, not just the words.** Listening for changes in pitch, volume, intensity, and speed of talking can give you clues to their real interest and engagement.
- **Notice micro facial expressions.** Just like in the facial coding techniques mentioned previously, people's immediate, fleeting expressions in their faces often give away their true feelings, even if they try to cover it up. Pay close attention though, as these come and go in milliseconds.

- **Put their words into context.** Always try to get at the "why" behind what a consumer is saying. What in their life might be causing them to think that way? Getting to know the person in more depth, such as seeing their home, hearing about their goals and dreams, and their plans for the future, can help you understand what's driving what they're saying.
- **Sometimes, just observe.** Just seeing how someone shops for something, how they use it, where they store it, how they handle it, and so on, can provide a wealth of information on how they perceive your product or service, without any words at all.

Takeaways

- Most market research today operates under a fundamental flaw that consumers are capable of telling you why they buy what they buy. It assumes consumers are conscious of these drivers and can explain them through language. But as much research has shown, this just isn't the case.
- The burgeoning field of neuromarketing has grown out of this issue and aims to use neuroscience to tap into the unconscious and true feelings of consumers. These techniques include fMRI, EEG, facial coding, biometrics, and

more. The Implicit Association Test (IAT) is a particularly promising method of unearthing unconscious associations with your brand.

- There are, however, many issues with current neuromarketing practices including their high cost, unnatural environments, and occasional exaggerated claims. They are also generally seen by creatives as creativity killers, rather than helping the creative process.

- Projective techniques such as collage building, image sorting, and personifications can be used in qualitative research to probe deeper, uncon scious feelings with brands. But note that interpretation of these results is difficult and key to understanding their applicability.

- It's also important to not just take what consumers say at face value, but to listen and observe behind and around the words they say. Look at body language, tonality, and facial expressions to get a better sense for what they are truly communicating.

CHAPTER 12

Innovating for the Unconscious

Developing New Products that Last

Let's face a fact: most new products fail.

Depending on who you ask, anywhere between 80–90 percent of all new product launches are gone within a couple years of introduction, and many even sooner than that. On top of that, it's also estimated that 80–90 percent of all startups fail as well. It seems we love to innovate, but we're just not very good at it.

Innovation has become such a buzzword lately that it has mostly lost its meaning. Every company is trying to be more innovative, or create a culture of innovation and entrepreneurship at their company. Every brand manager works hard on innovation for their brand. Despite all this energy and money focused on new product development, we still fail the majority of the time.

We all know about New Coke, but what about C2, the "mid-calorie" cola launched by Coca-Cola in 2004 with $50 million in advertising support? The product didn't fit a need and was too much of a middle ground to appeal to anyone, so it failed fast. And what about P&G, the master of product innovation, and their launch of Scentstories, a scent "player" modeled after a CD player? There was so much confusion around what the product was and why you would want it that it too died a quick death.

Product launches fail for many reasons. The market research may have been flawed, misinterpreted, or nonexistent. There may not have been a real need in the marketplace. It may be a copycat in an already saturated market. It may be too confusing or lack the education necessary to show consumers why they need it or how to use it. The timing may be wrong. It may not make sense for the brand. It may not be supported properly. Maybe the product doesn't live up to expectations. Whatever the reason, statistically speaking, your new product is probably going to fail. So what can we do?

In this chapter, we'll look at innovation through the lens of the unconscious mind and the Brand Fantasy to see how we can use a brand's associations to create better, longer lasting, and more desirable new product launches.

Innovation can be anything, as long as it strengthens your Brand's Fantasy

For starters, we should be clear on why we're innovating at all. The world has an endless supply of products, services, and ideas. If your idea adds to the noise and clutter, without something new to offer, does it really need to exist?

From the brand's perspective, new products should exist to strengthen your Brand's Fantasy. If it weakens the overall brand, it may provide a short-term sales bump, but will likely erode the brand in the long term. Brand extensions should add to what your brand stands for, making it more robust and deep. A new offering can solidify your place in the market, expand on your expertise, and help confirm your brand's associations.

As mentioned earlier, the classic book *Positioning* by Al Ries and Jack Trout states a strong opinion about this. They argued that a brand can only own one idea in the mind and should stick to that. Xerox used to own the copier market, but when they expanded into other office products, it was no longer clear what a "Xerox" was anymore and their previously strong and focused brand became diluted and lost meaning.

I think this is generally good advice: brands should stick to what they are good at and not spread themselves too thin. Trying to expand to be everything to everyone is a well known kiss of death. However, I believe they may have too narrowly defined what a brand is and what it can own. They stuck to the functional product—Clorox is bleach, Kleenex is tissues, Kodak was film. But when we look at positioning through the lens of the Brand Fantasy, perhaps the *feeling* of a brand is more important than just the product or category it's known for.

Many strong brands created line extensions that deepened and strengthened what they stood for, even if these were in different categories. For example, Nike may have once stood for sneakers only, but by building a brand around athletic performance they successfully expanded into all kinds of sports apparel and gear while maintaining the same core philosophy. This is why Apple can make many kinds of consumer electronics that all share the same Apple ethos and why Virgin can be successful in multiple categories—it always keeps the same rebellious spirit in anything it does.

You've probably heard of Toms Shoes. The trendy, casual, rustic footwear brand became famous in part for its buy-a-pair-give-a-pair program, where it donates a pair of shoes to people in need for every pair bought (like Warby Parker does with glasses). This makes their brand feel almost like a nonprofit. It seems like a positive social enterprise, alongside the likes of Habitat for Humanity or Teach for America.

Recently, Toms expanded into an unlikely new arena—selling ground coffee. Now, according to a traditional positioning mentality, this seems like a bad idea. Shoes have nothing to do with coffee, and those are two things I don't even want to think about being related. One smells great; the other, not so much.

However, because the Toms brand (separate from the product) is closely related to the idea of doing good, perhaps the coffee could enhance that part of the brand—and that's exactly what it does. The coffee is part of a clean water initiative, as they claim "with every bag of coffee you purchase, Toms will give one week of clean water to a person in need." The coffee is also organic, rainforest alliance certified, and single origin, of course. So although it still may seem odd for a shoe company to sell coffee, to me this adds to the Toms Brand Fantasy of being a company that prioritizes doing good. It makes it a stronger brand in some ways (although less of shoe experts) and could allow them to expand into other "doing good" categories as well.

Unfortunately, it seems like many new products, particularly line extensions, often dilute the brand, making it stand for less, rather than more. Brand managers are often pushed to find ways to grow and it can be tempting to expand an existing brand into related products. It's true that launching a new brand would be much more costly (in the short term, anyway), and the existing brand already has consumer trust. But this is too often at the expense of the long-term health of the brand.

For example, Haagen-Dazs launched a sub-line of ice creams in 2009 called "Five." These were meant to be simple, pared-down flavors that were made from only and exactly five ingredients (for example, milk, cream, sugar, egg yolks, and cocoa). I'm sure the folks at Haagen-Dazs believed this built on the consumer trends of wanting things to be more natural, simpler, and with easy-to-pronounce ingredients that you could find in your own kitchen. It fit well with the "real food" movement at the time.

But there were a few problems. Sure, it sounded nice and probably tasted great, but Haagen-Dazs isn't known for being healthy in any kind of way—even the "natural" or "simple" or "wholesome" kinds of healthy. It's an indulgent brand down to its rich, chocolaty core. So what did having a "Five" line add to the base brand? Nothing; in fact, it raised some questions, like what the hell else is in regular Haagen-Dazs? It also didn't provide anything new. In fact, many of the basic Haagen-Dazs flavors already had only five ingredients! You could also argue that it tried to make what is clearly an unhealthy dessert seem somewhat better for you, or even healthy, which would be misleading.

So although it fit with cultural trends, there was no consumer need, and it hurt rather than helped the base brand.

Many marketers tend to rely on a simple "brand fit" test: if the new product *can* fit under the parent brand, then that is good enough. But I suggest we raise that bar. New products shouldn't just fit with the parent brand, they should actively help strengthen and solidify what the brand stands for.

If it doesn't help the brand, it will hurt it.

Innovation can be the best form of marketing

Marketers tend to assume the best way to solve a brand problem is to market their way out of it. They think they have to *tell* consumers something to change their minds.

─────────────

Fun fact: the name "Haagen-Dazs" is totally made up to sound vaguely Danish, even though it doesn't mean anything in any language, and the Danish language doesn't even have umlauts in it. The brand was actually created by Polish-Jewish immigrants in the Bronx, New York. That's some clever branding to make the product feel foreign and fancy!

─────────────

But wouldn't it be better to prove it to them, rather than just tell them? Consumers today have very sensitive BS meters. They tend to distrust what brands say about themselves and instead look at what they do. Innovation lets you put your money where your mouth is.

Let's look at the example of the Gatorade G Series. Gatorade had originally been thought of strictly as a sports beverage meant for the field of play. But somewhere along the line, it slowly became more of an anytime drink, suitable for the couch potato as much as the athlete, and of course a hangover's best friend. This may have been good for volume and sales, but not good for the brand in the long term. Gatorade had lost much of its sports credibility.

They tried to market their way out of it. They had decades of well-known ad campaigns featuring top athletes. They were on the sidelines at the biggest events in American sports, with great product placement and press coverage. But still, many people thought of it mostly as a "sporty" drink that they could have with lunch, not a true piece of sports gear that helped athletes perform better.

Then (with the help of my former company, the brand and innovation consultancy Redscout) they began to expand their product lineup. The regular Gatorade product was meant to be drunk *during* sports, while you were sweating, to replace the fluids and electrolytes lost and to provide energy in the form of sugar. We realized that Gatorade could also give athletes' bodies what they needed not just during the game, but before and after as well. Those were very different occasions with different physiological needs, and athletes were using a variety of solutions in those moments.

Enter the G Series, a line of before, during, and after products with different formulations, each designed specifically for one of those occasions. The "before" product, named *Prime*, is a small energy shot that gives you the carbs you need to get going. The "during" product, called *Perform*, was the original Gatorade drink, and the "after" product, *Recover*, had protein to help your muscles rebuild.

Although the flagship product was unchanged, by putting it within this new context of a series, it gave it a much more specific purpose. It felt much more scientifically credible and fit for real sporting occasions, not the couch. The addition of the other products also made the Gatorade brand overall feel more scientific, legitimate, and for real athletes. They strengthened the brand, rather than diluted it.

They have continued to add to this line, which now includes "Prime" energy chews, a post game recovery shake, and a recovery protein bar. Though these products aren't huge sellers themselves, they serve to solidify and strengthen the brand overall.

Classic positioning theory might say that Gatorade is a sports drink and adding other products outside of drinks would weaken its position in consumers' minds as a great sports drink. Instead, the Brand Fantasy behind the Gatorade brand was strengthened as these products added to the brand's scientific sports credibility.

Use parent brands with caution

The Clorox Company makes Clorox bleach. They also make Hidden Valley Ranch salad dressing. These are two white, creamy liquids that are iconic in their respective categories. But I do not want to think about a bleach company making my salad dressing. A "Hidden Valley Ranch, from the makers of Clorox" would be factually true, but gross.

This is the joy that is brand hierarchies. Having a "parent" or "endorsing" brand can lend trust and credibility to another product or sub-brand, but it can also distract and cause confusion.

The brand Betty Crocker is well known in baking products, but the little red spoon logo bearing its name also appears on other products, such as Fruit Roll-Ups fruit snacks. Because the buyer for this product is typically a mom buying them to give to her kids, that Betty Crocker logo lends a bit of warmth, wholesomeness, and trust to what could otherwise have been easily seen as candy. The mom may not even notice the little Betty Crocker spoon in the corner of the box, at least not consciously, but it still might make her feel slightly better about the product, and feel slightly better about giving it to her kids as the treat in their lunchbox because of it. It adds a significant positive feel to the Brand's Fantasy and is more likely to pull her in.

On the other hand, there are also times when it's better to separate the brands. Think of Toyota and Lexus—separating the two allows Lexus to be a pure luxury brand, with all the status and elegance that comes with it. If Lexus made mid-tier cars like the Toyota Camry, it would pull the luxurious Lexus brand feel down with it. Of course, this isn't rational. The same company is still making both and the cars are unchanged, but how we think and feel about them changes drastically based on the very different brand perceptions.

The massive liquor company Diageo is a master of this. Most consumers don't know the name Diageo, because they don't use it as part of their brands at all; it's solely a parent company, not a brand. And that makes sense. I don't want to know that my Guinness Irish stout, which is about as Irish as you can get, is made by the same company that makes the quintessentially Jamaican beer Red Stripe. Those are totally separate brands with totally different Brand Fantasies, and they should be kept separate, even to the point of keeping the parent company behind both (and the Scottish Johnnie Walker, the Caribbean Captain Morgan rum, the London Dry Tanqueray gin, and so on) mostly hidden from consumers. They let each brand have their own distinctive, strong, and pure Brand Fantasy without muddying the waters—and oceans—between them.

Though it can be tempting to throw an "endorser" brand name on a new product to add familiarity, credibility, and trust to the new brand, marketers should ensure it adds to what the new brand is going to stand for, and doesn't take away from or confuse it.

As the world evolves, your brands need to keep up

Here's an obvious statement that we often forget: the world is constantly changing. Despite knowing this to be true, it seems many brands want to go back to what worked in the past, even if the world from that past no longer exists. We want to stick with what works, and if it ain't broke, we shouldn't fix it.

Although some products can make this work—Coca-Cola has been around for well over 100 years—most need to regularly update and refresh to stay relevant and meaningful in the ever changing world. Even Coca-Cola has had to launch Diet Coke, Coke Zero, and recently Coke Life to try to keep up with health and wellness trends.

Look at the story of vitaminwater. In the early 2000s, this brand was the epitome of cool (at least cool for the beverage world). It could be seen in the hands of trendsetters and celebrities, including the famous deal with rapper 50 Cent. Its standout package design was a mix of pharmaceutical black and white juxtaposed with the bright color of the liquid inside. And the witty on-pack copy gave the brand real personality.

The brand felt totally new and different, and created a whole new category of "enhanced waters." In a world that was beginning to question its love affair with soda, vitaminwater seemed like a healthier, but still fun and tasty, alternative. At the peak of its coolness, The Coca-Cola Company bought vitaminwater for the record sum of $4.2 billion.

Then the copycats came. There are obvious ones that rip off vitaminwater directly, but beyond that, a whole new category of "new age" beverages began to emerge. Take a walk down the beverage aisle at a Whole Foods, or even your standard grocery store, and you'll see a myriad of options of beverages that play some kind of health angle. There are flavored waters, functional beverages, many forms of iced teas, super fruit drinks, and so on.

In this new world of drinks, vitaminwater no longer stands out and actually feels more like a relic of a bygone time. The world changed, but vitaminwater stayed the same. And it has the long, slow decline in sales volume in the U.S. to show for it. The brand still feels like an early 2000s kind of cool. And though it may have appeared healthier than a soda then, in today's market where consumers are hyper-aware of sugar content, it no longer seems that healthy either. Its functional claims like "focus" and "energy" have also been called

---

You could imagine how vitaminwater could have changed with the times. Perhaps it could have begun lowering its sugar content (they added a "Zero" option with no sugar, but that may have backfired and caused more people to notice how much sugar was in the original). Maybe it could have added more powerful ingredients to truly live up to some of its functional claims. Maybe it could begin to feel more natural, with more natural ingredients. It did none of these and despite major marketing efforts and promotions, the product itself lost relevance. The Brand Fantasy died.

---

into question, and today there are many functional beverages that hit these benefits much harder. So what does vitaminwater have left to stand on? Not much.

But some brands have been able to evolve and weather different trends. Michelob Ultra, for example, was born out of the low-carb craze of the early 2000s and started out clearly positioned as a low-carb beer. However, the low-carb fad fizzled almost as fast as it came, and many low-carb products that had just launched were just as quickly removed. There were low-carb yogurts, ice creams, and even cereals and breads. But these were mostly pulled from shelves within a couple of short years.

Michelob Ultra, however, managed to evolve and stay a strong brand to this day. It repositioned itself from being a low-carb beer to the beer for healthy-minded, active, and fit people (or really, just weight-conscious people who aspire to be fit and healthy). They don't mention carbs much and don't give you much of a direct, product message anymore. Instead, they provide a very clear brand feel and personality. It says that, for those of you who see yourselves, or want to see yourselves, as fit and healthy (and who don't mind ridiculously watery beer), this is for you.

Even if the product doesn't change much, as is the case with a Michelob Ultra or Coca-Cola, the overall brand feel will still need to evolve to keep pace with the ever-changing tides of consumer tastes and cultural trends. Core values can and should remain, but the way they get expressed and live in the world will often need new faces to fit the new beliefs and the style of the times.

Today, most innovation may fail, but maybe that's okay. Failure is necessary for progress. Without trying, we'd never know what could be. But, hopefully, as market research methods improve, and we gain a better understanding for the unconscious influences at play with brand decisions, we'll keep failing at innovation—but we'll fail less and fail better.

Takeaways

- New products should help strengthen the base Brand's Fantasy, not dilute it. This can include stretching out into other categories, as long as the feeling behind the brand is strengthened and the innovation adds to the base brand.
- Innovation can be the best form of marketing; it proves something to consumers, rather than having to tell them about it and take your word for it.
- Parent or endorser brands can add or distract from a Brand's Fantasy, so use them appropriately and with caution.
- The world is always changing and your brand needs to constantly evolve to keep up. Don't assume what has been working will always work.

CONCLUSION

There you have it. My goal with this book was to bring out a new understanding of, and appreciation for, how brands live in the brain. I hope you've gained a new perspective on the amazing ways in which our brains work, how our conscious experiences are often misleading, and how we are not as rational or even as conscious as we think. I hope you'll now see brands in this new light and realize just how much power brands have lying beneath their conscious surface.

Most importantly, I hope you'll see how understanding the deep, hidden, unconscious associations with brands is not a creativity killer, but rather an inspiration to explore and bring out these hidden treasures. I find that a beautiful and liberating way to think about brand building, and I hope you do too.

My last hope is that we can continue this conversation. As science continues to chip away at the mysteries of the human brain, we can continue to refine and expand upon our understanding for how brands exist in it. If you'd like occasional updates on brain and brand science, and how you can apply them to your business, please stay in touch by joining my e-mail list and blog at *www.daryl-weber.com*. There you'll also find links to related videos, resources, and tools to help you seduce your consumers and uncover and build your own Brand Fantasies.

CHAPTER NOTES

Introduction

1. Al Ries and Jack Trout, *Positioning: The Battle for Your Mind* (New York: McGraw Hill Professional, 2001).
2. Kevin Roberts, *Lovemarks: the future beyond brands* (New York: powerHouse Books, 2005).

Chapter 1

1. Daniel Wolpert, "The real reason for brains," TED Talk, www.ted.com/talks/daniel_wolpert_the_real_reason_for_brains?language=en.
2. Hilke Plassman, et al, "Marketing actions can modulate neural representations of experienced pleasantness," Proceedings of the National Academy of Sciences, 105.3 (2008) 1050–1054.
3. N. Hodgson, "Citizenship Education, Policy, and the Educationalization of Educational Research," *Educational Theory*, 58 (4), 417–434.

4. A. Mantonakis, B. Galiffi, U. Aysan, and R. Beckett, "The Effects of the Metacognitive Cue of Fluency on Evaluations about Taste Perception," *Psychology*, 4 (3A), 2013, 318–324.
5. A.C. North, D.J. Hargreaves, and J. McKendrick, "The influence of in-store music on wine selections," *Journal of Applied Psychology*, 84 (2), 1999, 271–276.
6. Dan Ariely, *Predictably Irrational: The Hidden Forces That Shape Our Decisions* (New York: HarperCollins, 2010).

Chapter 2

1. Robert Heath, *The Hidden Power of Advertising: How Low Involvement Processing Influences the Way We Choose Brands* (Oxfordshire, UK: Admap Publications, 2001) and *Seducing the Subconscious: The Psychology of Emotional Influence in Advertising* (West Sussex, UK: John Wiley & Sons, 2012).
2. R.S. Lockhart and H. Craik, "Levels of Processing: A Retrospective Commentary on a Framework for Memory Research," *Canadian Journal of Psychology Outstanding Contributions Series*, 44 (1), 1990, 87–112.
3. W. Schneider and R.M. Shiffrin, "Controlled and automatic human information processing: Detection, search, and attention," *Psychological Review*, 84, 1977, 1–66.

4. D.J. Simons and C.F. Chabris, "Gorillas in our midst: Sustained inattentional blindness for dynamic events," *Perception*, 28, 1999, 1059–1074.

5. Sharon Shavitt and Timothy C. Brock, *Persuasion: Psychological Insights and Perspectives* (Boston, MA: Allyn and Bacon, 1994).

Chapter 3

1. Giep Franzen and Margot Bouwman, *The Mental World of Brands* (Henley-on-Thames, UK: NTC Publications, 2001).

2. Elizabeth Loftus and J.C. Palmer "Reconstruction of automobile destruction: An example of the interaction between language and memory," *Journal of Verbal Learning and Verbal Behavior* 13: 585–589, 1974.

3. Daniel L. Schacter and Peter Graf, "Implicit and explicit memory for new associations in normal and amnesic subjects," *Journal of Experimental Psychology: Learning, Memory, and Cognition*, 11.3, 1985, 501–518.

4. Jonah Berger and Grainne Fitzsimons, "Dogs on the Street, Pumas on your Feet: How Cues in the Environment Influence Product Evaluation and Choice," *Journal of Marketing Research* 45.1 (Feb., 2008), 1–14.

5. Gavan Fitzsimons, Tanya Chartrand, and Grainne Fitzsimons, "Automatic Effects of Brand Exposure on Motivated Behavior: How Apple Makes You 'Think Different,'" *Journal of Consumer Research* 35.1 (2008), 21–35.

Chapter 4

1. Paul Eckman, "Universal Facial Expressions of Emotion," *California Mental Health Research Digest* 8.4, 1970.
2. William James, "What Is an Emotion?" *Mind* 9, 1884, 188–205.
3. Antonio Damasio, *Self Comes to Mind: Constructing the Conscious Brain* (New York: Vintage Books, 2012).
4. Antonio Damasio, *Descartes' Error: Emotion, Reason, and the Human Brain* (New York: Penguin Books, 1994).
5. Erik du Plessis, *The Branded Mind: What Neuroscience Really Tells Us about the Puzzle of the Brain and the Brand* (Philadelphia, PA: Kogan Page, 2011).
6. Robert Heath, *Seducing the Subconscious: The Psychology of Emotional Influence in Advertising* (West Sussex, UK: John Wiley & Sons, 2012).

Chapter 5

1. Amos Tversky and Daniel Kahneman, "Judgment under Uncertainty: Heuristics and Biases," *Science, New Series*, 185.4157 (1974), 1124–1131.
2. Dan Ariely, *Predictably Irrational: The Hidden Forces That Shape Our Decisions* (New York: HarperCollins, 2010).
3. Jonah Lehrer, *How We Decide* (New York: Houghton Mifflin, 2009), 23.

4. Baba Shiv and A. Fedorkhin, "Heart and Mind in Conflict: The Interplay of Affect and Cognition in Consumer Decision Making," *Journal of Consumer Research* 26 (1999).
5. Daniel Kahneman, *Thinking, Fast and Slow* (New York: Farrar, Straus and Giroux, 2011).

Chapter 6

1. Daniel Dennett, *Consciousness Explained* (New York: Back Bay Books, 1992).

Chapter 8:

1. "The Bird, The Bike, and The Blue Behind Warby Parker's Brand," *Inc.* (magazine), July 10, 2012. http://us-events.hendricksgin.com/rsvp/event/form/emporium-general/hp.
2. "How Squarespace's CEO Pivoted to Scale for Millions," *Fast Company*, http://www.fastcompany.com/3030867/bottom-line/how-squarespaces-ceo-pivoted-to-scale-for-millions.

Chapter 10

1. "Case Study: Cadbury Gorilla," http://www.dandad.org/en/cadbury-gorilla/. https://en.wikipedia.org/wiki/John_Wanamaker.

Chapter 11

1. Martin Lindstrom, "You Love Your iPhone. Literally," *The New York Times*, http://www. nytimes.com/2011/10/01/opinion/you-love-your-iphone-literally.html?_r=0.

INDEX

INDEX

INDEX

ACKNOWLEDGMENTS

This book would not have been possible without the support, guidance, and help from many dear friends and colleagues. I must thank those that endured early drafts of the manuscript, and provided invaluable feedback and comments, including: Briana de Veer, Andra London, Brian Ballan, Justin Carr, Kyle Hugall, Emily Heyward, and Tiffany Graeff.

I also must thank Marc Andrew Stephens, the endlessly talented photographer and designer who helped put together the images in this book.

The neuroscientists who kept me on track by ensuring the science in this book properly portrayed the latest neuroscience understanding, without exaggerations or over promises, are Dr. Michael Treadway and Dr. Kartik Sreenivasan. Thank you to you both for your feedback and guidance.

Lastly, I want to thank my wonderful wife Jennifer, for her unwavering support and for being my voice of reason throughout this entire process.

ABOUT THE AUTHOR

Daryl Weber is a seasoned branding consultant whose work has influenced many of the best and biggest brands in the world, including Coca-Cola, Nike, Johnnie Walker, Gatorade, Pampers, and many more. He was formerly Global Director of Creative Strategy at The Coca-Cola Company, where he oversaw brand and communication strategy for many of the company's billion-dollar brands. Prior to that, he was Director of Strategy at the boutique brand and innovation consultancy Redscout, where he advised Fortune 100 companies on new product innovation and brand positioning. Weber has a BA in psychology from Columbia University. He resides in Atlanta with his wife, Jennifer, and son, Avi. You can follow him on Twitter @BrandedCortex.